STORY PLOTTING SIMPLIFIED

Story Plotting Simplified

By
ERIC HEATH

Boston
THE WRITER, INC.
Publishers

Printed in the United States of America

To

MARY

"The teacher who walks in the shadow of the temple, among his followers, gives not of his wisdom but rather of his faith and his lovingness. If he is indeed wise he does not bid you enter the house of his wisdom, but rather leads you to the threshold of your own mind. . . ."

Kahlil Gibran

(*By permission of Alfred A. Knopf, Publisher, New York.*)

PREFACE

MANY books have been written on the craft of writing, and quite a few less on the specialized subject of plotting. Some of them are outstanding; probably all are helpful, in one way or another. Each author has something to give of his own experiences in the writing field, as well as his individual conception of the writing art. We have personally received benefit from the ones that we have read and hope that the reader may be able to make the same statement in regard to this work.

The only claim we make to originality, after reviewing the mass of literature written on the subject of writing, lies in the author's own experiences in various fields of writing, and in the application of the Thirty-six Fundamental Dramatic Situations as compiled by Georges Polti, to modern plot usage. The author made his first analysis of these Situations some eighteen years ago in a book on photoplay writing. His initial study of Polti's masterly work caused him to believe that they offered the only *logical field* to draw upon for aid in plotting stories.

We emphatically do not want to go on record as advocating the systematic use of plotting methods or plot devices. At one time we originated a system of plotting stories through the shuffling of playing cards, upon which were printed various characterizations, situations, and so forth. The result was a rather interesting and entertaining device, but we soon realized the futility of it and the mechanical formulae which resulted. We do believe, however, that the methods worked out under the analyses of the Thirty-six Situations in this volume offer as feasible and workable a plan of achieving plot inspiration as any, but we also realize its limitations. Its chief attraction lies in the fact that it is based upon truly fundamental principles.

The Thirty-six Situations as analyzed in this work set forth the principles upon which story plots are based, but they should be studied, first, to gain a thorough knowledge of dramatic structure, and, secondly, for the inspiration they may lend in endeavoring to plot a story. When we say "story plotting," we include in all cases the plotting of stage plays, radio sketches and photoplays.

To use the Situations dogmatically as a source of all plots would be to mechanize creative endeavor and restrict imagination. The suggestions as to how they might be used in stimulating the imagination may be of untold benefit. But under no circumstances should any plotting help be relied upon for anything other than to attain a knowledge of plot construction and whatever inspiration it may have to offer for plot conception.

In defense of our contention that a knowledge of the Thirty-six Basic Situations is of the greatest benefit to the writer, we will make a statement that may strike some readers as being somewhat startling. *The Thirty-six Situations are the complete groundwork of all variations of story plots thus far conceived by mankind!*

If there are only thirty-six basic situations possible to use in story writing, is it not necessary and important that the writer should familiarize himself with these situations—the very backbone of his craft?

It will readily be seen that to adapt these Situations to modern usage is an intricate and difficult task. It is the aim of this book to lighten that burden somewhat, and yet, in view of the momentousness of the work, our interpretations of these situations and suggestions as to using them are submitted in all humility and with realization of their shortcomings.

CONTENTS

xi

PART I

THE FIELD OF WRITING
(Preliminary to Plotting)

CHAPTER I

THE PLOTTED STORY

ANY book on plotting is apt to be misinterpreted by some members of the intelligentsia and condemned because it teaches *formula.* Yet what would a motion picture or a stage play be without *plot?* Whether that plot is derived through the writer's building from a mere episode or idea, or the use of that much abused factor, "theme"—allowing the structure of the story to evolve naturally under its initial momentum—or whether the story is written after a carefully planned plot is first conceived—is immaterial. The formula is there just the same; and, within the scope of this work, that formula will be found duly classified under one or more of the Thirty-six Situations that follow! I welcome refutations of this statement from any of the "non-formulists."

It is true that some experienced writers create their stories without any definite plot outline and without any specific goal in sight. Many of them are numbered among our ablest authors. With this type of procedure, the story grows naturally through the characters, their relationships, and their objectives.

3

For us to advise the beginning author to write his story without any preconceived plot in mind would be like sending him out on uncharted seas in a row-boat. He would not have the knowledge necessary to know whether or not his story when finished would conform to a pattern acceptable to the editors and the reading public.

A pertinent query might be: How many successful writers are there who work without preconceived plot outlines, who do not have a knowledge of the principles of plotting?

In defense of all good books on plotting, we maintain that a knowledge of the technique of constructing stories is a requisite to the training of a writer. In order to disregard plot, it is necessary to *know plot*.

To proclaim that skill in plotting the story is all that is necessary to land it with the editors is, of course, to make an asinine statement. Even an excellent plot must be clothed with interesting incident, motivated by realistic characters and contain dialogue fitting the characters and circumstances.

The skilled writer can readily start his story with nothing more than a theme in mind. It might be timely here to define that word "theme." This is a difficult task. Many interpretations have been given to it. It has been defined to include the complete plot of the story; it is sometimes applied to the underlying idea of the story. Again, according to other interpretations, the headings of the Thirty-six Situations, such as *Revolt, Supplication,* etc. might properly be a *theme.*

We believe the best application of the word is to regard it as the "motivating idea" which is worked out through the development of the story. It is some thesis or proposition, the truth of which you wish to demonstrate to your reader. It is the abstract essence of what you want your reader to remember, after having read the story.

For example: The theme of "Dr. Jekyll and Mr. Hyde" is "The struggle between good and evil in the individual." The theme of the story of Disraeli is "The nation above the individual."

It will be seen then that a theme is hardly sufficient for the student-writer to use as a pier from which to launch his story. The same applies to a mere idea, or group of characters. Without conception of plot formula the chances are that the embryonic writer will wander and arrive nowhere.

The writer who knows the fundamentals of plotting is well aware that his basic structure as it is formed conforms to a pattern that will hold the interest of the reader.

We, personally, have found that we work best when we have a plot before starting to write, no matter how slender that plot thread may be. But whether to have a plot or not to have a plot before starting to write, is for the skilled writer purely a matter which applies to his own particular temperament and methods of working.

In certain fields of writing, such as the mystery story, it is almost essential to have the plot worked out in detail before commencing to write. Without a skilfully woven plot which withholds from the reader "Who done it?"—there would be no mystery.

Nearly all text books on writing will make mention of O. Henry. For years his technique represented the *ultima Thule* in the realm of plotting. But no longer does the surprise or "trick" ending hold sway as it formerly did. It still has its place in story construction and especially in the "short shorts," but by no means should the student feel that he must stun his reader by an unexpected twist in the end. A satisfactory solution worked out logically and without strain or coincidence should be the writer's aim.

Material

1. Sources of Material

While the Thirty-six Dramatic Situations and the treatments given to them, which comprise the main portion of this volume, offer an inexhaustible supply of ideas for material to use in story, novel, play and radio writing, some additional comments will be made here for the further guidance of the writer.

The sources from which the writer may derive his material are so numerous that it would be futile to attempt to enumerate them. In every corner and crevice of life, stories are lurking. In the life of every person, no matter how uninteresting he or she may appear, are stored enough experiences to fill many volumes. Life is one vast treasure-house of ideas, but in order that they may be used, dramatic insight must be brought to bear upon them.

The creative mind is the mind that *perceives,* that looks beyond the surface of things to the deep, underlying significance. To the person who exercises real imagination, nothing is commonplace; nothing is monotonous or boring or meaningless; every day teems with a myriad of incidents that have story potentiality. Even the keenest observer misses a large percentage of the drama that is taking place round about him. On the fifth floor of a New York apartment house a gay party may be in full swing, while, at the very same time, a lonely girl, having struggled in vain against the cruelties of life, is in a room on the seventh floor taking poison. The postman who brings a letter to your door may be concealing by carefully expressionless face, the agony he is suffering because, the evening before, his daughter ran off with a scoundrel.

The writer has the whole gamut of human emotions at his disposal. His domain includes everything that life affords. Providing he has *vision, sympathy,* and *sincerity,* he will be able to beautify the familiar, the commonplace; to illumine the dingy and sordid.

2. *Heart Interest*

The human emotions form the basis of all art. We reiterate that the story, play, poem, or any other form of what purports to be artistic writing, must therefore deal with these fundamental emotions, else it is mere form, an empty shell. A page of statistics differs from a page of fiction in that the former involves figures in certain mathematical arrangements; the latter, the thoughts and feelings and impulses of mankind.

"Heart interest" implies the establishment of a bond of sympathy between the character in the story and the spectator, such a close bond that the suffering, the joy, the triumph of the one is shared vicariously by the other.

This may be considered one of the most important elements of the story, novel or play. The reader or audience will be captivated, if the characters of the story are so lifelike, so admirable and lovable that the appeal they make is irresistible.

Heart interest depends primarily upon the characters; their relationships with other characters in the story; their admirable qualities that are set forth through their actions.

Readers want to have their emotions played upon. They want to be made to *feel;* otherwise, the story will leave them cold and entirely unmoved.

Remember that you are writing *about* human beings, *for* human beings. This does not imply that sentimentality is what is needed. But if your characters are merely dead puppets to you, if you cannot see them and hear them and understand them, your story becomes a formal document, which, like the page of statistics, leaves the emotions untouched.

3. *The Love Element*

Because it is a fundamental and universal force, love is one of the chief emotions, whether the word be used to designate the love between man and woman, or the love of the individual for nature, art, humankind. It plays a vital part in all the relationships and situations in which man finds himself. It touches the life of everyone in some measure.

We might go so far as to say that most stories include some expression of this emotion, and please understand that we do not mean necessarily, love between man and woman. Even in the field of the "pulps," in a story with no feminine interest whatever—merely, we will say, a case of a policeman running down a crook—there is a subtle element of love—love for humanity through protecting it from vicious influences.

True Stories

In speaking of material, a word or two about "true stories" is important, because the beginning writer so often starts off his writing career by writing the story of his life, or of episodes which he has actually experienced.

Maybe it is just as well to get this autobiographical type of material off your chest in the beginning. Until you do, you won't feel satisfied. The chances are your life experiences *do* offer a source for many stories, but in most cases true happenings are either *too true* to *seem true,* or they are lacking in the elements of drama or comedy so necessary for entertaining reading.

We do not advise the student writer to slant his work for the "true confession" magazines. The so-called "true story" is very likely to have been written by a professional writer. In fact, adhering to our determination to leave no truths unrevealed, we, personally have sold quite a few stories to the true confession magazines—mainly at times when the exchequer was low and some quick money was needed for the landlord.

Nevertheless, the fact remains that you have so much competition with both amateurs and professionals in the field of the true story, that to devote your time to this type of material is apt to be futile and non-remunerative. If you *must* write a true story, write it, but do not make this type of writing your goal. Aim for the very highest in your chosen work and even though you make a lowly beginning, select a type of fiction that will at least lead definitely toward a worth-while objective.

Formula Stories

We shall frequently refer to conventional formulae in discussing the Thirty-six Situations. In order that the student may have a better idea of our meaning, we will attempt to give broad definitions of various types of formulae used in the field of the "pulps."

Magazines in the higher brackets, such as *Cosmopolitan, Saturday Evening Post, Ladies' Home Journal, Red Book,* and the like, also publish "formula" stories. In other words, all of their fiction material comes within the boundaries of a pattern, although generally a very broad one. This is the reason why it is so essential for the beginning writer to study the medium for which he has decided to write.

Because of the almost unlimited variety of material published in magazines such as those mentioned above, it is quite impossible to give any concise definitions of the patterns underlying such publications. A very good rule to follow, however, is to study the advertising in such magazines and get it firmly in mind that no story that is in any way prejudicial to the advertisers in such mediums will be considered for a moment. The advertiser is a vitally necessary factor to the success of the magazine, and has to be considered as such.

In *Cosmopolitan,* for instance, there will be found many advertisements of schools and colleges. This is an indication to the writer that any story of a salacious nature, or one which might contribute to the undermining of youthful character, would not be acceptable.

Some magazines now carry full page liquor advertisements. We doubt if you will ever find in these any articles or stories advocating the return of prohibition. Neither will you find stories antagonistic to cosmetics manufacturers; stories which set forth the evils of the credit and collection methods in force with some of the large and influential installment concerns; nor the bunkum attached to many well-advertised nostrums.

A very broad definition of the formulae for all such class magazines is, then, that stories should be clean and uplifting, carry no elements objectionable to the advertisers, stress the greatness of our American civilization and optimism for the country's future. This results in the publication of stories romantic in character, adventurous, humorous, and dealing with the love theme cleverly and in a more or less sophisticated manner. Stories involving every-day human problems have a wide appeal in these publications.

As will be gathered from the above, propaganda stories are definitely out; also stories belittling any nation, any creed or race; stories promulgating a new social order; stories which deal with sex in too straightforward a manner. To sum it all up, in writing for these publications, keep your material innocuous, but make it clever, sufficiently sophisticated, and above all, create characters that are real and lifelike.

Returning to the "pulps": here we have quite well-defined formulae. Each magazine has an established pattern, and unless the submitted yarn conforms to that pattern, it will receive a prompt rejection. The following will give the reader some idea of the formulae involved.

Western Story Magazines

The Western pulp yarn generally concentrates the action on the struggles and motives of one central character, a cowhand. He may have a confederate, or "stooge," quite often an older cowhand, either a humorous or cantankerous individual. This associate serves usefully because he is someone with whom the hero can discuss plans to be pursued in the struggle against the antagonistic factor. He also comes in mighty handy when the hero gets into a tight spot, by coming to his rescue in the nick of time.

Of course the hero is a super-man when it comes to rapidity in drawing a six-gun, riding a horse and using his fists. And his confederate is no slouch in these accomplishments either.

It is hardly necessary to state that the antagonist, or

"bad man," is capable of almost anything—murder, larceny, abduction—anything but rape. The sex angle must be soft-pedaled. The heroine must always be a clean, fearless sort of person, and yet always dependent upon the hero in times of stress. Where there is a woman associate of the "bad man," she is hard, dishonest and calculating, and can endeavor to use her wiles on the hero. But she must never stoop to real sexual naughtiness.

If a woman is brought in as a protagonist in the Western story, it invariably ends up with a marriage in sight for the hero and heroine. A few Western story magazines demand that little or no emphasis be given to the feminine element.

The Love Story Magazines

Under this heading we refer to the clean type of love story, and are not referring to the risqué or pornographic type of publication.

The formula for the love story generally calls for the heroine to be sweet and pure, and a person who adores "he-men" and romance. The appeal must be eternally youthful. Stories of middle-aged or elderly people (who, strangely enough, may still feel romantic!) seldom have a chance with this type of magazine. Sex is, of course, the dominating motif, but sex in its clean, moral aspect. Some melodrama is allowed and a happy ending is definitely essential. Avoid writing anything which will require the reader to place any undue strain on his mentality. Love stories are aimed to give "escape" to the adolescent girl, or vicarious thrills to females who have been thwarted in their love lives and have not as yet found that big, tall, dark man!

Detective Story Magazines

There was a time when magazines dealing with detective-mystery themes concentrated more or less on skillfully worked out plots, with real finesse on the part of the detective. The trend at present, however, is away from stories involving clues and astute detective work. Action seems to be the watchword. The hero is, of course, practically infallible, and capable of getting out of any tight situation, either by cleverness or by pure muscular effort. If he whips three scoundrels single-handed, so much the better. In other words, the physical aspect, in addition to the mental, is stressed more than ever before in detective story magazines.

Naturally, there have to be several murders—sometimes it is almost wholesale slaughter. Don't worry too much about overdoing it. That mild-mannered clerk with the spectacles, poring over that "Daring Detective" magazine is wallowing in blood—and liking it! Probably he wouldn't really care to decapitate a chicken for his Sunday dinner, but there is a primitive streak in him somewhere deep down, maybe going back as far as his caveman ancestors—and he can take all the bloodshed you want to give him—on paper.

There must be a thread of plot, but it does not need to be entirely logical or carry a sense of realism, so long as you keep the hero moving and fighting and keeping after the antagonists until they are duly slaughtered or placed in durance vile.

Generally a feminine interest is required. She serves as the noble, harassed being for whom the hero struggles, and he either passionately or mildly falls in love with her in the middle or toward the end of the story. Quite often, he mistakenly thinks she is in cahoots with the villains, which hurts him very much because she seems to be such a nice sort of kid!

As in love stories and westerns, soft-pedal the sex angle. Salacious details of the villain trying to seduce the girl have no place in this type of yarn. The struggle must be clean—and bloodthirsty. But whatever you do, don't worry the hero, whether he be a detective, a reporter, an amateur scientist, or what have you, with tiny bits of hair, special brands of cigarettes, measurement of footprints and other "Sherlock Holmes" devices. These belong in the field of detective books, and not in the action type of mystery yarn.

Adventure Magazines

Again we must have the clean, supple, quick-witted hero, generally slim-waisted, bronzed from tropic suns, and willing to dare anything for the sake of a woman or a cause. Please understand that we are not belittling this type of yarn. Some of the adventure magazines in the pulp field publish superior types of stories, splendidly written and often worthy of recognition as real literature.

Nevertheless, the formula is there. In his conflict with renegades, smugglers, natives, mutineers, etc., the hero must be honorable and law-abiding. The purpose for which he is struggling must be a just one which meets the approval of the reader.

Quite often there is a strong feminine interest; sometimes, however, little or none, depending upon the magazine and its policy. The heroine, as in the case of all pulp stories, is a most deserving bit of femininity, and the better looking she is, the more she will appeal to the masculine reader of this type of story—and as a rule adventure stories do not appeal so strongly to feminine readers. It's a good rule to have the female antagonist a graceful creature, with soft, olive skin, and great burning dark eyes, filled with shrewdness, devilishness, or lies—whatever applies best to her character.

The antagonist generally falls into a rather stereotyped category: He may be a trafficker in slaves; a revolutionist; a clever and polished thief; a spy; white chief of a native tribe; a plantation owner; a murderer; a pirate; or any dynamic personality who carries on his evil ways in a colorful or exotic locale.

It is an accepted rule in dramatic conflict that the more clever and astute the villain, the more interesting will be the conflict, and to the same extent will the hero have to demonstrate his worth. In adventure stories the antagonist should be keen and clever and prepared to take advantage of the physical characteristics of his habitat, in order that he may duly demonstrate his evil courage and his alert, yet distorted, mentality.

Other Classifications

The field of pulp fiction encompasses so many varied subjects that space forbids entering into a discussion of each one of them. The aforementioned classifications have the widest range of readers and consume an enormous amount of material. In addition, we have aviation, sport, fantastic, ghost, terror, risqué, true confession, and numerous other types of pulp magazines. Each follows a formula and it behooves the beginner to make a careful study of this formula before attempting to write for such media.

Characterization

Before studying plotting, the writer must realize that without true-to-life characters, interesting personages, no plot can retain its interest and suspense. If the principal character of your story is a decidedly insipid, flighty sort of an individual, purely artificial in his thoughts and actions, a character created without feeling or proper visualization, your plot will be equally superficial and lacking in realism. After all, a plot is based on the struggles of your characters; it is dependent largely upon the human element. How then, can you evolve an interesting or dynamic plot without interesting and dynamic characters?

The starting point of story writing, we believe, is coming to be generally recognized as lying in the field of characterization. A prominent leader in the motion picture world recently declared that upon characterization rests the entire future of the screen art.

The first and cardinal rule is to *know your characters*. When you know them, you will be able, with careful thought, to determine just how and why they would do certain things under given circumstances. Carry on a mental existence peopled with characters of yours. Study the relationships that exist between them; continually establish new and more interesting relationships between them.

After you *know* your character, place him or her in certain circumstances. How would the character act? Just what would be his reaction? What would *your* reaction be if you were placed in those circumstances? What are the emotions and impulses that go with that character's make-up—his being? If he were unjustly accused of theft, for instance, would he strive for retaliation, revenge? Would he try to clear himself, or seek aid from friends? Would he extricate himself through "pull" or through his own acts? Suppose now, he found out his daughter wanted to marry a man who had accused him? What would he do?

Knowing the life history, the development of each of your characters, you will be able to explain *why* a character has an admirable or a despicable trait, and to show *how* his heredity and environment fostered that trait.

For instance, if, in a story, you wish to have a young girl fling herself into a gay Bohemian life at the first opportunity, you will not merely state that she is an impulsive and reckless girl, but knowing your character and the past influences in her life, you will explain this by calling attention to the training she received from a strict, Puritanical aunt, during many years of restraint, so it would be quite natural that, the reins being loosened, she should react from a rigid environment by going to the other extreme.

It would be illuminating for the student-writer to study some of the old motion pictures, read some of the old books and plays, such as *Ten Nights in a Barroom,* Horatio Alger's works, etc., and note the tremendous advance that has been made in this matter of characterization. In such pictures, plays and books, the characters were almost nearly all "types." There was the heroine, the very personification of goodness and beauty; the hero, the most manly, courageous, and clean-minded of his sex; and the villain, the most dastardly, sneaking, cowardly, cruel wretch imaginable! Utterly unreal, these characters were merely "puppets" to be manipulated by the writer of the story. Their actions could be predicted, and for this reason, they would be very tiresome to the more discriminating audiences and readers of today.

Real, lifelike characters, "neither all good nor all bad," are necessary to endow a story with poignancy and vitality. Create natural, human characters, and you will find them doing interesting things—in fact, building the story for you out of themselves and their relationships to one another, provided you have a definite objective for them. If you start your plot with good characterization, the material and the theme for your story will present themselves to you through character development, aided and abetted possibly by being guided into situations which you may be able to develop through using the Thirty-six Situations which follow.

The real difference between the "pulp" or action type of fiction, and the material used by the magazines in the higher brackets, lies largely in characterization. In the former, the characters are more stereotyped as a rule and the reader becomes more interested in their actions than in their personalities. Their spoken words may be natural, and true to the types depicted, but the reader of action fiction is not apt to care particularly whether they exchange brilliant repartee or not.

And yet to presume to vilify the action type of story would be to attempt to destroy one of the best means of "escape" provided for the reader who is either too fatigued mentally to tackle a more subtle form of literature, or whose educational background precludes his getting anything out of it.

Motivation

All the action, dialogue and descriptions involved in a story should be initiated by the characters. In other words, the ambitions, desires, impulses of the characters, as these characters are brought into relationship with each other, should form the story basis.

This implies that the first task of the story writer is to *introduce his characters* and show the relationships existing between them. When the characters have been introduced and brought into relationship, the writer must keep the *motives* of each character clearly in the mind of the reader. Show *why* each character acts as he does, and keep each one true to his own personality. Let the motives for all actions be well defined and convincing.

Have your characters "work out their own salvation." Do not force them into artificial situations, for such situations never ring true. And this may serve as a warning in your study of the Thirty-six Situations for plotting purposes.

While "chance" or "coincidence" often does play a part in real life, it denotes weak dramatic construction to rely upon this factor in working out a plot. It is far more convincing to have the motivation *spring from the characters themselves.*

While on the subject of "coincidence," it is timely to reiterate that every so-called rule can be blasted successfully if done skillfully. We get a great deal of enjoyment ourself out of reading the works of Harry Stephen Keeler, and we doubt if there is any greater exponent of "coincidence" than Mr. Keeler. And yet he uses coincidence so expertly and with such unexpectedness that it is enchanting to follow the mental processes involved.

Coincidence can generally be avoided. For example, suppose it is important for purposes of your plot that two characters meet at a railroad station. Instead of having such a meeting "just happen" to occur, it would be better to have it brought about as a result of the planning of some third character, who is anxious that this meeting take place.

If you wish to get rid of a character, do not go to the trouble of having him killed "accidentally" in a train wreck. This is too "convenient" a way to eliminate him from the plot. Instead, maybe some antagonistic character can "fix it" so that he is sent to South America, or some other place.

Do not resort to elaborate roundabout motivation. Keep it as simple as possible. Remember that your characters supply all the motivation that is necessary.

Chapter II

THE STUDENT'S LABORATORY

Prior to a concentrated study of the Thirty-six Dramatic Situations for plotting purposes, it has been thought advisable to introduce here some ideas for practice work on the part of the student. It is also recommended that the student procure some good works on the general subject of writing and study them in connection with his application of the Thirty-six Situations. To gain the viewpoints of a number of teachers on the art of writing is bound to be of the greatest aid in studying plotting.

1. *Material*

In order to facilitate your practice work, some suggestions regarding *Material* are here offered. They may appeal to you or they may not. Of course a very poor story as well as a very good story might be constructed with each of these suggestions as a starting point. The value of your story will depend upon the way it is developed. After a thorough study of the Thirty-six

Situations, endeavor to use them as a basis for working these ideas into story form.

Naturally, all ideas given in "The Student's Laboratory" are for practice purposes. However, since no two writers will ever develop the same theme in the same way, and since it is true that there are *only thirty-six basic situations* in all story literature, there is nothing to stop you from striving to construct salable material out of any ideas presented.

(1) The intense struggle between idealistic forces and mercenary forces in the world of big business and high finance.

(2) The dramatic conflict of the patient, persevering fishermen of the Maine coast (or any equivalent locality) against the invasions of unscrupulous traders, who upset their simple and humble mode of living by breaking down the barriers that shut these little communities off from the outside world.

(3) The attempts of any character, brought up in a hostile environment, to conquer the limitations of that environment and rise superior to them.

(4) The antagonism between a group of characters, life-long dwellers on Mississippi "house boats," and some "land" characters that they meet.

(5) The conflict of some master intellect, struggling for good, against the forces of evil, through clever and convincing detective work.

2. *Themes*

(1) There is an intermingling of good and bad qualities in every individual.

(2) The struggle to attain recognition and prominence in life is, in many cases, more worthwhile than the recognition and the prominence attained, for success often means moral bankruptcy.

(3) The weak are often stronger than the strong.

(4) Unselfishness can be gained through suffering.

(5) Discontent is a gnawing, destructive force, affecting rich and poor, young and old, and often leading to sin and disaster.

(6) "We often pause at the guarded gate, and pass the gate ajar." (Stuart Walker)

3. *Characterization*

The suggestions which follow do not purport to be fully developed characterizations. They are just sketches that might serve as a basis for characterizations. They are given to stimulate the student's imagination and to help him to characterize.

(1) Mrs. Mira Crissy leaned far down over her glass candy case to give the little boy his nickel's worth of lollipops. She took her trade very seriously. She figured out every ounce of her wares to the eighth of a cent. She grasped in her toil-worn fingers a chewed-off stubby lead pencil with which she "entered" sales in her

"ledger." Her business was high finance to her. Sometimes, at night, when she took off her old alpaca dress in the loneliness of the back room that was her home, she vaguely wished that her Uncle Thomas had not left her the store. It was such a burden.

(2) Young Bob Darell was the only one who did not hold himself in high esteem. He discounted the opinions of his college mates and of admiring "girls." While he hurriedly tied his tie that morning, he looked into the mirror at his slick, light hair, his tanned, glowing face, with its cheery eyes and good-natured mouth, and suddenly became serious for a moment, and muttered: "You cad! That's all you are—a cad!"

(3) Miss Vance closed her desk wearily. Another school day over. How her head ached! How she wished she might have an evening of relaxation, instead of correcting papers in her cramped little sitting room. While she fumbled into her hat and coat, she found herself actually crying. And then she remembered. This was her fortieth birthday. And at forty, people are "middle-aged" and uninteresting. Of course, she did not *look* so very old, but why then had not her eighteen year old niece invited her to go on that skating party? She had wanted to go—oh, how she had wanted to go!

(4) Evelyn Haddon was the only girl in the room with *shoes* on. Her quick eyes darted from one pair of satiny slippers to another. How can one dance in

shoes? And such shoes! She had gotten them at a bargain, rather than come in her old ones, that were down at the heel. Her hands, lying in her lap, were clenched. She drew her feet up beneath her skirts, as far out of sight as possible. Yet if she told them that her father was wealthier than the father of any other girl there, they would not have believed her.

(5) Roger Clinton, the "aluminum magnate," was tired of his riches, tired of his house, tired of his servants, tired of his·wife. He wanted just one thing— to get away from business that seemed to be crushing him spiritually, and to rest. He had neither comfort nor pleasure from his fortune. Others used it, but he did not. He had the hustle, the worry, the responsibility. Even his Sundays were not his own. Suddenly, the old determination showed in his handsome, furrowed face. He decided in one moment, that he would put an end to an intolerable situation; with one masterful, keen stroke, he would cut himself loose.

(6) She was a wild little thing, and nobody knew where she belonged. It was said that the Widow Crane had adopted her, but she and the widow had had a falling out, and Janie (yes, that was her name) had left. It seemed hardly possible that she could be sixteen as she said she was. She told that to the judge of the juvenile court when she was caught stealing, and she surely would not have been foolish enough to try to fool the judge! He was a strange sort of bird himself,

though. He *liked* Janie. Some say, though you never can tell for certain, that he took her to his home and there she is living in style, a sister to the judge's own innocent little daughter!

PART II

PLOTTING

APPLICATION OF THE THIRTY-SIX FUNDA-
MENTAL DRAMATIC SITUATIONS AS COM-
PILED BY GEORGES POLTI TO MODERN PLOT
USAGE.

Chapter III

THE THEORY OF PLOTTING

Before taking up the Thirty-six Fundamental Situations, which are, as stated previously, the basis of all plots used in stories, novels, photoplays, stage plays and radio sketches, the student-writer should have some knowledge of the definition of plot, the dramatic unities and how to create a story situation.

Further, a word of advice and admonition is needed to bring home to the writer that although the Thirty-six Situations set forth the principles upon which plotting finds its inception, they should be studied first, to gain a thorough understanding of dramatic structure, and, secondly, for the inspiration they may lend in aiding him to plot. To use them dogmatically as a source of all plots would be to mechanize creative endeavors and restrict the flow of imagination. The suggestions as to how they may be used in stimulating the imagination may be of untold benefit. But under no circumstances should they be relied upon, any more than various other plotting systems, mechanical devices or books, for everlasting inspiration.

Once the student understands the fundamental principles of plotting, he should draw upon his own imagination for ideas and themes for stories. When he has brought to the surface of his mind an idea that he feels will offer the nucleus of a good plot, he should develop it, work it out in a way that he is convinced will bring it within the scope of truly interesting and entertaining reading.

Concentrate on the Thirty-six Situations as treated in the following for the knowledge they may give you of plotting, and for ideas and suggestions for themes and outlines, but don't seek to find in these pages that lifelong foundation of plot material which will give you all you need to build interesting stories. It may be there, but there is only *one* place to search for real creative thought, and that is in your *own mind*. The ideas that spring up through creative thought will be the ideas that have that little touch of inspiration which will make them the nuclei of truly human, realistic and novel plots.

What Is a Plot?

According to Webster's dictionary, a plot is defined as follows:

". . . . The plan or main story of a literary composition."

This is not very helpful. The plan might be a simple narrative thread, that, if woven in beautiful literary style into a story, might be acceptable to the editors of certain "class" magazines, but entirely unacceptable to the publishers of popular types of fiction, or the script buyers for pictures, radio or stage. Class publications, such as *Harper's, American Mercury, Coronet,* etc., represent a very minute portion of the publishing field and for any writer to try to achieve financial security through his writings by appealing entirely to these publications would be unwise.

However, a great many pleasing narratives ramble on leisurely through the lifetime of the characters, giving incident after incident, lengthy conversations and philosophical reflections. In the novel, there is, of course, a fairly wide field for this narrative type of material, provided it is very well written.

Again, for the stage, there are exceptions. Some of Bernard Shaw's plays, for instance, are dependent on brilliant dialogue and abstract ideas.

And yet, to those aspiring to write deep and thoughtful narratives without striving for plots in the true sense, a knowledge of plotting is essential.

An artist may paint a most fantastic picture which utterly departs from all conventional standards, but you may be sure that the artist first learned the art of painting through a depiction of "type" studies. So, if your ambition is to write literature of a deep or classic nature, first learn the principles of plotting as applied to the type of literature read by eighty percent of our reading public. You must understand fundamentals before you reach the heights.

But let's get back to the meaning of plot. Just what is a plot? It is safe to say that if you asked this question of a dozen well-known writers, you would in each case receive a different answer. At least that has been our experience.

"Our definition of a plot is: *A dramatic premise growing out of which the characters move through one or more situations to a climax and solution.*" Ordinarily the second situation should be of greater intensity than the first, the third greater than the second and so on, and the climax or crisis should be the highest. When we speak of intensity, we mean that the *suspense* should be increased as the story progresses—the outcome or solution should be more and more in doubt.

And now what is the meaning of a *situation*? We believe that a situation might aptly be called a state of circumstances wherein the principal character or characters are placed in a "predicament" or dilemma. For example, we give you the rough outline of a story of our own, which although more or less conventional, happens to serve the purpose of pointing up situation and climax admirably.

Jim Doyle, an engineer, is at the throttle of his engine as he pilots a night passenger train toward its destination. His heart is heavy because his young brother, Danny, is seated in one of the coaches in the rear, handcuffed to a deputy sheriff, on his way to the penitentiary.

Jim finds he is a little behind time. He calls to his fireman for more steam. As he does so, he looks around and finds himself facing Danny. Danny quickly explains that he escaped from the deputy sheriff by hitting him over the head. He demands of his brother, Jim, that he slow down the train, so that he can jump and make his escape.

From this premise a situation, or "predicament" has been evolved. Jim is faced with either refusing to carry out his brother's request and making sure that the boy is carried on to the penitentiary, or with slowing the train, abetting his brother in defiance of the law as well as going against the rules of the railroad.

What shall he do? He is confronted with a conflict between love and duty. Truly, he is in a predicament —faced with a dramatic situation!

Let us go on with the story:

Jim has always loved his kid brother. The boy has kept wild company and made a mistake in forging a check, but that can't take away the affection he has for the boy. As he thinks of this, there is a jerk on the signal cord. The deputy sheriff in one of the rear coaches has returned to consciousness and has pulled the cord to stop the train.

Jim breathes a sigh of relief. Now he *has* to slacken speed.

Danny leaps from the train and hurries off into the night.

Note that there is a slowing down at this point in the tension or suspense. The boy got away—Jim was relieved from his present situation. Now it is necessary to go forward to the next situation, which is, in this story, the climax or culminating point.

Danny after fleeing across the fields comes to a highway. He spies a parked car, steals it and carries on his get-away in the automobile. He comes to a small town and notices the depot clock. Jim's train, bearing the deputy sheriff, will be due in less than half an hour. He realizes that at this station the sheriff will give the alarm and warn the police to watch out for him. He stops the car. To his relief he sees a milk train pulling out and going in the opposite direction from the oncoming train bearing his brother and the deputy. He dashes across the tracks, clambers aboard one of the freight cars and relaxes.

It is a stormy night and rain descends in veritable torrents. While rounding a rocky cliff, the milk train on which Danny is riding is wrecked by a landslide. The wreckage is strewn over the tracks on which the train bearing Jim and the sheriff, as well as many passengers, is due to arrive within a few moments.

Danny, not badly hurt, crawls from the wreck. The train crew have either been killed or injured. No one can stop the oncoming train except Danny. What shall he do? Stay there and save the train or flee? If he stays, he will inevitably be captured and be forced to serve a long term in the penitentiary. If he does not save the train, his brother, riding in the engine cab, may very likely be killed or injured.

Danny, this time, is in a predicament or dramatic situation. The reader is in a state of tension waiting to know what decision Danny will make. Danny has been drawn as a pretty tough young fellow, disdainful of practically everything of moral value.

The story has now reached its climactic (in this case, the second) situation.

Danny, of course, saves the train and gives himself up. The reader is happy to know that he did the nobler thing, and the denouement or solution has been reached.

The Dramatic Unities

Prior to an intensive study of plotting and the Thirty-six Situations, it is necessary to say a few words about the dramatic unities.

The most satisfactory way to distinguish between material which is purely narrative and material which is dramatic, is by testing the material to determine whether or not it violates the law of dramatic unity—which resolves itself into three phases, the unity of time, the unity of place, and the unity of action. This law was formulated by Aristotle, and has been proven, after all these years of practical application, one of the most *useful* of guides in constructing the compact, closely knit plot for the short story, stage play, screen play or radio sketch.

The novel has, of course, been left out of the above category, due to the fact that the dramatic unities need not apply to the novel, which can have plots, and sub-plots, gaps in time, many changes of locale, and so forth.

The *unity of time* requires that the time during which the action of a plot takes place be as short as possible; with no "jumps" in the action, no long time lapses necessitating new beginnings. The plot should start with a definite group of characters and carry those characters through a few months, or preferably, a few weeks; all the drama being concentrated into this short space of time and the plot moving rapidly and continuously.

The *unity of place* requires that the "locale" or setting where the action of the story transpires, be confined to one locality, if possible, and never extended to more than two or three. A constant changing of the "locale" makes a plot rambling and disjointed. For example, if a story begins in America, then the scene shifts to India, then to Egypt, back to America, and to India again, while the various portions of the plot unfold, there can be no compact, cumulative dramatic upbuilding; the characters are separated; the effects are scattered, and an audience or reader is apt to become hopelessly confused. Likewise, if a story concerns a great many different households in the same city or town, and the action skips from one to another, the same confusion will result.

The *unity of action* requires that a plot be "all of a piece." Three or four different stories, each with its own group of characters and its own special line of development, must not be grouped together as one story. There must be one definite theme developed; one definite set of characters to work out this theme; and one definite goal toward which all the action tends.

It must be clearly understood that a great many good stories DO violate the unities. The law should not be regarded as a hard and fast one; it allows of exceptions. Of course the unities apply much more stringently to the stage and screen than to fiction. And yet in stage plays and in the photoplay, these laws are continually being violated. The fact remains, though, that the student-writer may very well keep the unities in mind in his early work.

The Thirty-six Dramatic Situations

In his scholarly work, Georges Polti formulated the law: There are only thirty-six fundamental dramatic situations, various facets of which form the basis of all human drama.

We have been asked many times by student-writers: "Can it be possible that there are only thirty-six situations and that this comparatively small number of situations comprises the entire field of plotting in literature?"

The answer is invariably "yes." To the skeptical it is suggested that they recall any book, story, play or piece of literature of a fictional character. Let them resolve such work to its skeleton plot basis. Apply this basic plot to the Thirty-six Situations of Georges Polti and you will find that it inevitably comes under one or more of the situations listed.

Take, for instance, *Romeo and Juliet,* probably the outstanding dramatic masterpiece of all time. Its basic plot theme might be said to be "a free union impeded by the opposition of relatives"—a subdivision of Situation Number Twenty-eight—*Obstacles to Love.*

And then again, take Galsworthy's play, *The Mob.* This comes under subdivision B (1)—*Revolt of one individual, who influences and involves others,* a nuance of Situation Number Eight—*Revolt.*

The above are classic examples of plot theme applications. Let us take the basic plot of the famous modern book, *Gone With the Wind.* In Scarlett O'Hara's devastating love life, we will find the theme of the book coming directly within the category of the

Twenty-eighth Situation—*Obstacles to Love* and the war theme coming under Situation Number Nine, *Daring Enterprise,* subdivision No. B (1)—*War.*

The principal difficulty in using and applying the Thirty-six Situations to modern story plotting lies in the rather subtle and classic style of presentation by Georges Polti. It has been the endeavor of the author to overcome these obstacles and present the Thirty-six Situations in a manner by which writers can apply them to advantage in conceiving plots. Whether or not the result is completely satisfactory, it is obvious that a close study of the Basic Situations will be of untold benefit to the embryonic writer and edifying to the professional craftsman.

We will now take up each situation, first setting it forth as conceived by Polti, then analyzing and dissecting it for the practical application of the plot builder.

CHAPTER IV

FIRST SITUATION

Supplication

(The dynamic elements technically necessary are: —*A Persecutor, a Suppliant* and *a Power in Authority,* whose decision is doubtful)

Famous usage of this First Situation:—*Madame X.* (Bisson)

THIS first situation is basically dramatic and apt to lead toward tragic lines of thought. However, it should be understood at this starting point that although many of these fundamental situations appear to have no usage except in the more morbid types of material, this is not the case. This situation can be aptly applied to comedy. The familiar formula of a young man in love with a girl whose father is bitterly opposed to the match is a very old application of this situation, in plots of a humorous nature.

Such terms as "Persecutor," "Suppliant," and "Power in Authority" may be given a wide delineation, and it is only in this way that a practical application can be made of these Situations. *A too literal translation of the*

*Thirty-six Situations is apt to make them more a matter
of academic interest than of practical use in the field of
writing.*

Our procedure throughout will be to first give you a
practical method of using the elements of the Situation
in modern plotting. We will then take up each subdivision of the Situation, and discuss it.

Practical Application of Situation Number One

The dynamic elements of this situation, *Supplication,* are, as stated under the heading, "A Persecutor,"
"A Suppliant," and "A Power in Authority."

For the assistance of the student in his attempt to
use the Thirty-six Situations in a practical way and to
bring suggestions for plots to his mind, we give below
a list of possible factors which might be used. An
explanation of how it may be used and enlarged upon
will follow this list.

A PERSECUTOR	*A SUPPLIANT*	*A POWER IN AUTHORITY*
Detective	Criminal	Judge
A husband	A wife	Her lover
A "mercy killer"	An invalid	The law
The Law	A boy and his dog	Pound-master
A husband (surgeon)	His wife's lover	The wife
The Squire (Old melodrama)	The farmer	Farmer's daughter

A PERSECUTOR	A SUPPLIANT	A POWER IN AUTHORITY
Two business men	Wife of a thief	Greed
Man of wealth	Suitor for his daughter's hand	Girl's mother
An explorer	A native	A native god
Ranch owner	Cowboy	Cattle rustler
Owner of gambling house	Embezzler	Owner's daughter
Commander of Outpost of Northwest Mounted Police	A Mounted Policeman	A fur trapper
A mother	A child	The father
Superintendent of Reformatory	His daughter	A male inmate of institution
A sea captain	A sailor	A storm

(Note here that personalities do not necessarily have to be factors. This also applies in the case of "Greed," above.)

A PERSECUTOR	A SUPPLIANT	A POWER IN AUTHORITY
A salesman	Another salesman	The buyer
A collection manager	A creditor	Legal technicality
Football coach	Football player	Coach's daughter
A senator	Office seeker	A child
Drouth	A farmer	Water
Army captain	Soldier	Cowardice
Doctor	Interne	Superintendent of hospital
{ A beautiful girl	An ugly man	Wealth }
{ Wealth	A beautiful girl	An ugly man }

(Note how the elements may be reversed to attain entirely different angles.)

A PERSECUTOR	A SUPPLIANT	A POWER IN AUTHORITY
Starvation	Old man	Relative
Lottery	Winner of lottery	Sudden wealth

(The above might seem confusing, but imagine the winner of a large sum through a lottery being beset by many worries attendant upon sudden wealth. The lottery is really the persecuting force to the winner and the power of the money he receives rules his destiny, which is in doubt. This point is illustrated to stress the broad application which can be given to these elements.)

A taxi owner	A taxi driver	A gangster
Department store manager	A shop girl	A customer
A wild beast	A hunter	A natural catastrophe
Insanity	Relative of insane person	Another relative
A wife	Man in love with her	Her husband

The above list could be extended endlessly and the student is urged to create new applications of the elements or factors. He may, if he likes, type the above factors on thin cardboard, doing the same thing with the factors given with each of the following Situations. By spreading out these cardboards before him and combining the factors of one Situation with another, he will attain an unlimited variety of plot suggestions.

As stated elsewhere, *imagination must be brought into play*. Take any one of the above listed elements, reading across the page. Here's the result from the first combination, written off just as it came to my mind—consuming about three minutes in the process. Very rough and conventional, no doubt, but certainly a nucleus for a plot.

We take the very simple formula given above of "A detective" (Persecutor); "A criminal" (Suppliant) and "A judge" (Power in Authority). A boy pleads with a detective or officer of the law and insists that he is innocent of breaking into the judge's home. The judge has been out of town. He returns and learns of the boy's arrest when the officer found him in the judge's basement. The judge takes the role of humanitarian, discovers that the boy had been lured there by the members of a rival boy's gang, in order to punish him for having thrashed their leader. The boy has lived up to his code of "not snitching," but through clever psychology the judge wheedles the truth out of him.

Now let's place some of the factors in different juxtaposition. In other words, instead of reading across the page, let's jump around. For instance, we will make "A sailor" the Suppliant, "A detective" the Persecutor, and "Football coach's daughter," the Power in Authority. Seems rather mixed up, doesn't it? But let us suppose the sailor is in love with the Football Coach's daughter. The daughter learns that one of the players on her father's team, who has been in love with her, plans on "throwing the game" to avenge himself because she has turned him down, and also to gain money from a gambler in order to impress her. The daughter, a loyal booster of the team and believer in her father's pre-eminence as a coach, calls upon "the sailor" to help out. She is in love with the sailor and he with her. The sailor takes matters in his own hands and tries to abduct the crooked member of the team. A detective steps in on the sailor as he is about to get the crooked player safely out of the picture, and arrests the sailor. In order to protect him the girl confides in the detective and he holds the football player, the antagonist, until the game is over, the home team triumphs and all ends well.

All very crude, but it demonstrates the ease with which a plot of sorts can be worked out. To obtain suggestions for really worthwhile plots, *much thought and imagination must be used*. There is absolutely no royal road to plotting!

We have deliberately refrained from working out any skillfully conceived plots from the above factors. This would be to demonstrate the use of the Situations as to their ultimate possibilities, and give the impression that the mechanics involved are revolutionary in their scope. This is not the case. To work out a worthwhile plot through using the factors requires real creative thought and no dogmatic adherence to the "types" indicated.

However, for the writer needing and seeking inspiration through plotting aids, we believe that the above simple and practical application of the Basic Situations is about as good as could be devised, and will not necessitate the study of a bewildering array of material, or endless shuffling of cards, or turning of wheels, or what have you. And another thing—the above factors *are based on proven fundamentals!*

Below are a few sketchy outlines given to indicate to the student how this First Situation can be used in many plots:

1. A prosecuting attorney, endeavoring to convict the hero or heroine of a crime, with the latter appealing to the court on the basis of moral issues rather than legal.

2. The good offices of a priest or clergyman appealed to by a criminal pursued by an officer of the law.

3. A wife revealing her love for another man in order to save him from the husband's vengeance.

4. The "mercy slaying" of an invalid with the suppliant appealing to the code of humanity as against the technical application of the law.

5. A penniless boy pleading for the life of his impounded dog. (In this idea, the boy, of course, is the Suppliant, the pound-master is the Power in Authority and the law represents the Persecutor.)

6. A husband, a surgeon, is called upon to perform an operation on his wife's lover, the wife being the Suppliant, the husband's hatred representing the Power in Authority.

Again, at this point, it must be impressed upon the student that even a "state of mind" may be used as an antagonistic force. In item 6, the husband's state of mind might well represent the Power in Authority. Just what the husband's decision will be, takes care of the qualification following the third element of the triad—"A power in authority, *whose decision is doubtful.*" The husband, of course, in this case represents both the Persecutor and the Power in Authority, with the wife as the Suppliant.

7. (An ancient melodramatic version). The hardhearted Squire, who holds the mortgage on the old homestead (the Squire being the Persecutor), offering to cancel said mortgage if the farmer (Suppliant) will force his daughter to marry him, (the daughter being the Power in Authority, inasmuch as she can refuse and ruin her old daddy or agree and save the old rickety farm-house with all the pigs, cows and chickens walking around it.)

This example gives an idea of how completely Georges Polti encompassed the entire range of plot elements!

8. (Humorous) Two men in financial straits have a valuable jewel which is amply insured. A thief enters, ties them up and takes the jewel. Gleefully the men plan to collect the insurance money, which is far more than they could have sold the jewel for. The thief's wife enters in the midst of this jubilation and

returns to them the jewel which she forced away from her husband. In this outline, the wife is the Suppliant, the two men are the Persecutors (from her standpoint) and the Power in Authority is represented by the decision the two men may make—whether to forget the whole thing, in spite of their chagrin, or send the man to jail.

All of the above rough outlines were worked out rapidly through a use of the factors listed above. Again note outline No. 8, and in your future use of the Situation factors, do not overlook the fact that not only personalities may be used as dynamic elements, but mental states of the characters, human emotions, Nature, animals, and so on, may be considered as usable factors under one or more of the three headings.

Subdivisions of Situation Number One

It is not necessary to go into any great detail in regard to the various subdivisions of this or any of the following Situations. However, it is very necessary to list them and discussions in some cases will be of benefit.

SUBDIVISION A (1)—FUGITIVES IMPLORING THE POWERFUL FOR HELP AGAINST THEIR ENEMIES.

This subdivision of the First Situation offers excellent opportunities for the writer of plays and screen stories, if he is able to apply new variations. Frequently, it can be used in conjunction with Situation Number Two—*Deliverance*.

Simple examples: (1)—Residents of the "dust bowl" in the Middle States (fugitives from disaster) appeal to the Government for aid (The Powerful), to save their land.

(2)—The members of a yachting party are shipwrecked on a deserted island. They kneel and pray to God to bring them help and save them from starvation.

This example is deliberately given in order to again impress upon the student that the application of the word "fugitives" in its true meaning does not necessarily apply. In this example, the members of the yachting party are fugitives in one sense of the word. They are fugitives from the wrath of the elements. The "Powerful" to whom they appeal is, of course, God. Their "Enemies" are represented by the elements of hunger and cold. A more literal variation of this could be worked out by having the island inhabited by savages. One of the sailors has a radio sending set which he puts in one of the life boats. He endeavors to contact the authorities on a near-by island to send help. In this version, there is a clear-cut delineation of all the elements of the Subdivision.

SUBDIVISION A (2)—ASSISTANCE IMPLORED FOR THE PERFORMANCE OF A PIOUS DUTY WHICH HAS BEEN FORBIDDEN.

It is obvious that this subdivision was of more value

in classic drama than it is in modern, for pious duties have not the importance in the daily life of today that they had in former times. It has been used in a number of plays dealing with Indian life, in which a character appeals to a power in authority for permission to bury his dead.

The writer must be warned that unless this subdivision is given a subtle and very careful treatment, it is apt to produce too morbid an effect.

It is, in fact, suggested to the student that no attempt be made to use this subdivision in modern writing. This represents an instance, among several others, where an ancient or classical usage is almost imperative. It may fall naturally into some classification of present day writings, but we believe it would be a waste of time for the student to strive to use it in plotting.

SUBDIVISION A (3)—APPEALS FOR REFUGE IN WHICH TO DIE.

The chief use of this Subdivision of Situation Number One is in melodrama, in which a character—usually one of the unsympathetic faction—seeks a refuge from his pursuers. It is essentially tragic and morbid.

Example: A man, deeply in love with a girl, discovers that he has contracted leprosy. He goes away to a leper colony, and seeks admission to stay there until death overtakes him.

This example represents a tragic situation conceived from this Subdivision. For the student of plotting, it is enlightening, inasmuch as it is indicative of the fact that a true dramatic situation can be built on elements other than the conventional "hero, heroine and villain." Here we have a situation in which the great antagonistic force is "disease."

SUBDIVISION B (1)—HOSPITALITY BESOUGHT BY THE SHIPWRECKED.

This has commonly been used in sea stories, and is a concrete example of the admonition that in itself this Subdivision offers no real plot. It can only be used by being combined with one or more of the other basic situations. In the example below such combinations are given for the greater understanding of the student.

A ship which carries a number of college girls is wrecked on a far northern coast. The inhabitants of the section in which the girls find themselves are all men. In seeking hospitality the girls find themselves confronted by two elements—a group of men hungry for feminine bodies and a group of men yearning for the love and companionship of a good woman. Here we have a plot based upon this Subdivision with an added variation of the Twenty-fourth Situation, *Rivalry of Superior and Inferior.*

SUBDIVISION B (2)—CHARITY ENTREATED BY THOSE CAST OFF BY THEIR OWN PEOPLE WHOM THEY HAVE DISGRACED.

Situation Twenty-seven, *The Discovery of the Dishonor of a Loved One,* is closely allied to this situation.

This is primarily a dramatic or tragic situation, although, as stated before, practically all of the Basic Situations can be twisted to attain comedy or humorous results. The above subdivision was used recently in a motion picture, in a comedy fashion, as follows:

The hero, scion of ancestors steeped in classical music, turns to jazz composition, to the horror of his family. Although, technically speaking, he did not exactly entreat his relations to understand that jazz paid more money than the classics, they came to his rescue when he was sued for plagiarism by showing that most popular musical numbers have their basis somewhere in the classics. In his efforts to get out of his predicament, there was an element of entreaty involved and we believe through a liberal interpretation of this situation, as should be done with practically all of the Basic Situations, this plot comes within the scope of this Subdivision.

SUBDIVISION B (3)—EXPIATION, THE SEEKING OF PARDON, HEALING OR DELIVERANCE.

Stories involving this particular subdivision, fall in the category of death-bed confessions, in which the character who is dying appeals to those he has persecuted for pardon. This use has been almost exhausted through constant repetition, especially in pictures. However, the idea itself is worthy of a more varied and original treatment.

It is difficult to use this Subdivision as a complete plot basis. It may be used in conjunction with the Third Basic Situation, *Crime Pursued by Vengeance,* the Fifth Situation, *Pursuit,* and a number of others.

Example: A man commits murder. He flees from the law. His conscience torments him with increasing force until he is faced with almost complete madness. He goes to the confessional and upon advice of a priest gives himself up to the law. He finds that the person against whom he committed violence has recovered and has forgiven him his crime.

The above plot brings in the situation of *Pursuit,* also the Subdivision now being treated, as well as Situation Number Thirty-three, *Erroneous Judgment,* and Number Thirty-four, *Remorse.*

It might be to the point here to explain that we use suggestions which occur to us, such as the above crude plot outline, rather than quoting situations from more or less familiar books and stories. Many books on writing use examples from well-known literature, but we have found that no matter how well read the student may be, it is utterly impossible for him to remember very many of the works quoted. We feel, therefore, that more can be gained through crude but applicable examples than by the more generally used method.

SUBDIVISION B (4)—THE SURRENDER OF A CORPSE, OR OF A RELIC, SOLICITED.

While this Subdivision was used many times in classic drama, it is of little value to the writer of modern literature, except in the case of "horror" or "fright" stories.

SUBDIVISION C (1)—SUPPLICATION OF THE POWERFUL FOR THOSE DEAR TO THE SUPPLIANT.

Modern dramatists and story tellers have used this Subdivision sparingly and so it offers a good opportunity for future use. As in previous Subdivisions, it does not offer the basis for a plot in itself. It must be combined with other Situations.

Using a hackneyed theme, merely to stress points to be brought out: A labor leader incites some factory men to strike. In the melee that follows the labor leader injures a captain of the police. He is engaged to marry the captain's daughter. She pleads with her father to refuse to prosecute. The captain, in turn, is faced with following out his duties as a law enforcement officer.

It should be noted in the rough outline above that the story has reached a true crisis, or high point of tension. What will the captain do? Will he give in to his daughter, or will he rigidly enforce the law, regardless of the fact that by so doing he may break her heart?

Whatever solution is conceived (and new twists and angles *can* be given to the oldest plot formulae!) the writer of such a plot will bring about a proper denouement or solution, technically speaking.

The situations involved by using Subdivision B (4) as a nucleus are as follows: Situation Number Eight— "Revolt" (where the labor leader incites the workers to strike against improper working conditions); the Thirty-fourth Situation, *Remorse,* (for the injury to the father of the woman he loves); Twenty-third Situation, *Necessity of Sacrificing Loved Ones,* (the daughter's decision to sacrifice either her father or lover, as the writer may decide); and the solution or denouement might bring in Situation Number Twenty-one, *Self-Sacrifice for Kindred,* should the captain fail in his duty and refuse to file a complaint against the labor leader.

The above plot outline, by going further into detail, might bring even variations of other basic situations. It offers a spendid example of the necessity for blending the elements embodied in a number of basic situations to contrive a strong plot, and a splendid example of *what not to do in modern plotting,* unless you can give it that "novel twist."

SUBDIVISION C (2)—SUPPLICATION TO A RELATIVE IN BEHALF OF ANOTHER RELATIVE.

One of the most poignant uses of this subdivision has been in stories dealing with divorce wherein a suppliant child brings about a reunion between mother and father. As a general rule, this nuance is used in a subsidiary capacity in relation to the main plot.

SUBDIVISION C (3)—SUPPLICATION TO A MOTHER'S LOVER IN HER BEHALF.

This subdivision of Situation Number One naturally tends towards more or less morbid or risqué plot bases. However, for the stage it offers possibilities. For the screen it is probably out, due to censorship restrictions.

Example: A daughter realizes that her mother's lover is slowly breaking down her beloved parent's morals—dragging her to ruin. In order to save her mother from such a fate, she offers her body to the lover if he will give up his attentions to her mother.

It will be noted that this also brings in a very definite interpretation of the Twentieth Situation, *Self-Sacrifice for an Ideal*. It is interesting to note how various situations in any plot contrived fit into one group or another among the Thirty-six Situations! As a test, the writer should take any story of his own and search through the basic situations. By doing so, he will find that he has *actually* used some nuance of at least one and probably more than one of the basic situations!

We have gone into detail in analyzing and treating this First Situation in order that the student may have a clear conception of how to use the situations that follow. Our treatment of the remaining thirty-five situations will be more brief. However, by now the student should have a good groundwork to proceed.

Chapter V

SECOND SITUATION

Deliverance

(Elements: *An Unfortunate; a Threatener; a Rescuer*)
  Famous usage of this Situation: *The Count of Monte Cristo* (Dumas)

For the information of the student it might be well, in introducing this Second Situation, to stress the necessity of having proper dramatic elements in order to build a novel and interesting plot. The above elements, "Unfortunate," "Threatener" and "Rescuer," offer a splendid example of striking plot elements or factors. In every plot there must be an antagonistic force (the Threatener) of some kind to allow for tension and suspense. If your leading character languidly strolls through the fields, for instance, dwelling upon the beauty of the far-flung golden carpet of wheat, utterly carefree and ambitionless, he might incur interest through some splendid prose or narrative—but not until that character comes up against an obstacle or is confronted by an antagonistic force (Threatener) will he offer any real dramatic interest.

To create a situation suitable for modern story writing, your leading character or characters must be confronted with adverse conditions, must struggle to gain their objectives against opposing forces, be those opposing forces individuals, Nature, their own weaknesses, or evil tendencies, animals, mechanisms, or what not. The more serious the predicament they find themselves in through such opposition, the more intense will be the interest of the reader in wondering how they will extricate themselves, and what results will be attained after they do so.

As a simple example in every day life of how interest may be aroused through a mild element of suspense or wonder: Let us say that you go to the railroad station to watch the trains come in and go out. (Or if that isn't enough motive, you go there to meet a friend who is due in on the five forty-five). You notice a man carrying a heavy valise hurrying towards a train which is just about to pull out. He mounts the lower car step, looks up at the car window and around at the station. The train starts off slowly. The man, instead of climbing to the platform of the car, swings out and leaps from the train. He hurries off through the station and disappears.

Wouldn't you have a mild curiosity, a sense of wonderment at least, to know what made that man, so evidently in a hurry to board that train, actually mounting the first car step, then get off the train and rush away? If you have the proper writer's imagination, you would probably wonder whether he was a fleeing criminal and saw a detective watching him through a window of the car; or whether he was leaving his wife due to a violent quarrel, and at the last moment could not go through with it, and had to hurry home to ask forgiveness—and so on and so on.

Why must we have situations and crises in plays, screen stories and fiction? (Speaking of popular types of material, of course—or the average vehicle). Because situations are necessary to arouse the emotional interest of your spectator or reader. To entertain, you must play upon the emotions of your reader.

You must take the human emotions of love, pity, hate, jealousy, greed, sensuality, etc. and play upon them as you would caress the strings of a harp. If you have depicted interesting characters and involved them in entertaining situations, your reader will, as he reads, be mentally living right with them, almost "inside" of the character delineated. If your principal character is being tortured mentally, so will your reader be tortured. If your heroine, an heiress, is deeply in love with a poor young man, your reader at the moment will also have a nice feeling toward that young man too and sense a keen disappointment when that young man marries a penniless shop girl, whom he does not love, on the theory that "the poor should always mate with the poor."

But now to go back to our Second Situation—*Deliverance.*

This Situation is, in a way, the reverse of the first situation, in which the unfortunate appeals to an undecided power, whereas here an unexpected protector, of his own account, comes suddenly to the rescue of the distressed and despairing.

This Second Situation embraces a very broad category. A great many of our modern plays, pictures and fiction stories could aptly be said to be based upon this situation. In fact, our present day Relief Program has the same elements, i.e., the Jobless (Unfortunates), Poverty (Threatener), and various Governmental agencies, such as the Works Progress Administration, taking the place of the "Rescuer." It may seem far-fetched to use a social system as a dramatic premise, but the example will serve to explain the far-reaching possibilities of this Situation.

Naturally, the Situation as stated, implies a happy ending. If the rescuer is at hand, it is obvious that the unfortunate will come out all right. Therefore, the situation seems to be of no particular value from the tragic standpoint. It does, however, offer a splendid basis for comedy. In fact, from a review of a number of Charlie Chaplin's old comedies, it will be found that they are based on this identical situation. Charlie, in most of the old pictures, was a very unfortunate individual. The Threatener was to be found in the "heavy," always depicted as an enormous man with glowering visage. He not only played heavy parts, but he was chosen to *look* the part. The rescuer quite often was the heroine—in one case, we recall, a Salvation Army lassie.

We will digress again, to go into the matter of comedy plotting and comedy elements.

In the broader forms of comedy, especially as applied to stage and screen, there is generally little mental conflict. In this type of comedy, it is usually a matter of swiftly moving action and clever repartee. But whether the comedy be broad or light, the factors are just as clearly defined as in drama and the conflict between them just as keen.

Comedy may be designated as the sort of story in which the situations, for the most part, are humorous and amusing. The primary aim of comedy is to amuse the reader or spectator, to cause smiles, chuckles, laughter. In the modern field of comedy, there are a number of classifications:

1.—Burlesque, which is based upon extravagant or exaggerated situations and broad dialogue. In burlesque, it is generally a matter of *caricature,* rather than *character*.

2.—Situation or farce comedy—in which most of the humor is found in unexpected twists in the plot, the leading characters being precipitated rapidly from one predicament to another of a ridiculous nature (sometimes of a melodramatic type). The dialogue of farce comedy is generally humorous through application to the situations.

3.—Satirical comedy. The premise of satirical comedy is to hold up for ridicule some of our most sacred institutions and beliefs. Bernard Shaw is probably our greatest modern exponent of satirical comedy.

4.—Comedy-drama. This is a combination of both comedy and drama, with many of the situations serious and even harrowing, but never disastrous or actually tragic, the story throughout being written in a vein of light seriousness, and at frequent intervals, turning into situations of laughter and gaiety.

It is an accepted fact that no matter how tragic or serious a play, story, or picture may be, it should have its moments of lightness and humor. Our advice to the student is to endeavor always to spice his dramatic or tragic efforts with a dash of comedy or humor. The reverse applies to the humorous work. Nothing is more impressive than the bringing in, in a comedy vehicle, of a touch of pathos or drama. A swift transition from the humorous to the tragic is sometimes a shock to the audience, but in that very fact itself it serves to hold the interest and heighten the tension.

Continuing with the Second Fundamental Dramatic Situation—*Deliverance,* we shall again give a list of suggested factors, as we did with the First Situation. The factors in this situation may be blended and placed in juxtaposition with the factors of the First Situation. This also applies to the factors listed for all of the following situations. Make a practice of combining the various Situations and the factors involved. It is not necessary to adhere to the dynamic elements of a single situation.

AN UNFORTU-NATE	A THREATENER	A RESCUER
A man in love with a prima donna	A gangster	The prima donna
Migrants	Poverty	A farmer
A poor musician	His wife's father	Success
A dog	A man bitten	A boy
A fortune teller (girl)	The law	Wealthy man in love with girl
A race horse owner	Owner of race track	Owner's daughter
An Indian	Racial prejudice	Achievement
A share-cropper	Owner of land	Share-cropper's daughter
A negro preacher	A Voodoo cult	Prayer
A child	Kidnapper	The G-men
A murderer	Relative of victim	A priest
An actress	Loss of prestige	Inspiration through new-found love
Two married men	Two girls	Their wives
A student	Blindness	Science
A spy (man)	Another spy (man)	Third spy (woman)
A deer	A mountain lion	A dog

As an example of the use of these factors, let us take the first group listed. The Unfortunate is a man who is in love with a prima donna. He has, unwittingly, antagonized the leader of a gang of crooks (Threatener). He goes on a hunting trip, making his headquarters at his mountain lodge. His sweetheart, the prima donna (Rescuer), learns that the gangster is on his way to the lodge to kill her sweetheart. She knows he will be listening in to the broadcast of the opera in which she is to sing the leading role that night. When she appears on the stage, she calls a warning to him over the microphone, instead of singing the opening lines of her song. He hears her, of course, and overpowers the gangster.

Each combination of factors should be worked out into plots along the lines of the above, and then if one appeals particularly, it should be reworked until a satisfactory plot is obtained.

Then follows the process of visualization, of getting each character clearly in mind; decision as to the type of locality to be used, whether a small town, a big city, a farm, a seaside resort, Hollywood, New York, Paris, or whatever seems most applicable to the plot formula. After that comes the creation of incidents and a general settling in the mind of the entire story structure.

You are now ready to proceed with the actual writing of the story. This will call for a beginning that will hold the attention of the reader. The first few paragraphs of a story are probably the most important. How many times have you gone to a library, opened a book and glanced at the first page? If there was something on that first page that caught your eye, you would probably take out the book to read.

Many methods may be used to gain attention in the first few lines of your story. The use of conversation between two characters sometimes may work out satisfactorily. A striking description of a house, a countryside, or some material object, may do the trick. Depicting the principal character or characters in action at the opening offers a very good way of getting into a story, especially if it is to be of the "action" type.

You have your plot structure well formulated and you know exactly what you are going to have your characters do, the various situations or predicaments in which they will be placed and how the whole thing will end. Your next work now lies in your portrayal of character action, revealing your characters as truly human in their traits, putting words in their mouths that are in harmony with their characteristics, and in creating color and atmosphere through brief but vivid descriptions of people, places and objects.

When we speak of "color and atmosphere," we mean that you must convey to the reader a feeling that the environment in which your characters have been placed is *real*. He can picture it in his mind, imagine for the moment that he too exists in such a place. He is given the strong impression that the characters "fit in" to their surroundings. He experiences vicariously the subtle influences of the locale and its people—as does your principal character.

For instance, if your heroine lives in a cheap boarding-house, the reader will react to the depressing effect it has upon her, when he knows that she is a girl who is used to life on a large farm. He receives this impression poignantly when he reads of her standing at the window and looking out at a backyard filled with ashcans, drying clothes and mangy cats—yearning for the far-flung wheat fields that surrounded her old home.

We give below a tabulation of the elements of a story and the manner in which these elements are conveyed to the reader:

Environment (Established through description)

Characterization (Description, action, dialogue)

Dialogue

Action

Color-atmosphere (Conveyed through dialogue and/ or description)

Situations (Action, dialogue, description)

Climax (Action, dialogue, description)

Denouement or solution (Action, dialogue, description)

It all seems quite simple, doesn't it? But to put all

of these theories into practice is a very different matter. That is something which the student must do for himself, and the reason why the statement is made that no one can be *taught to write.*

Subdivisions of the Second Situation

A—APPEARANCE OF A RESCUER TO THE CONDEMNED

Frequently, as in many melodramatic photoplays, when an innocent character is about to be executed on circumstantial evidence, this Subdivision has formed the basis of the climax. This usage is both sensational and hackneyed, and the situation admits of many far more interesting and appealing developments.

B (1)—A PARENT REPLACED UPON A THRONE BY HIS CHILDREN.

This Subdivision is frequently found in the classics.

B (2)—RESCUE BY FRIENDS, OR BY STRANGERS GRATEFUL FOR BENEFITS OR HOSPITALITY

Polti's comment in regard to this Second Situation is illuminating. He says: "We see, by a glance over these Subdivisions, what our writers might have drawn from the Second of the Situations. For us, indeed, it should possess some little attraction, if only for the reason that two thousand years ago humanity once more listened to this story of the Deliverer, and since then has so suffered, loved and wept for the sake of it. This Situation is also the basis of Chivalry, that original and individual heroism of the Middle Ages; and, in a national sense, of the French Revolution. Despite all this, in art,—if we except the burlesque of Cervantes, and the transplendent light flashing from the silver armor of Lohengrin,—in art, as yet, it is hardly dreamed of."

CHAPTER VI

THIRD SITUATION

Crime Pursued by Vengeance

(Elements: *An Avenger* and *a Criminal*)

Famous example of this Situation: *The Emperor Jones* (O'Neill)

DIFFERING from Situations One and Two, this Situation has but two dynamic elements—the third factor in the dramatic triad is not given.

The Situation is basically dramatic, although it has been used many times in comedy, generally, however, of the farce-comedy type. In such comedies the protagonist is often the "criminal," although probably only a criminal from the viewpoint of the antagonist or "heavy."

In order to use the procedure as given in the preceding two Situations, it is necessary to include a third element and make a dramatic triad. The only feasible element, we believe, would be "A Power in Authority," in the broadest usage of that factor:

PRACTICAL APPLICATION OF SITUATION NUMBER THREE

AN AVENGER	A CRIMINAL	A POWER IN AUTHORITY
The law	A criminal	Detective
	(Mystery story formula)	
A father	His son-in-law	His daughter
The accused	A murderer	Skilled detective deduction
	(Variation of detective-mystery formula)	
A lawyer	His partner	A stenographer
A violinist	The robber of his Stradivarius violin	A concert
An author	A plagiarist	Author's wife
A man in love	His rival	The woman
A motion picture producer	A director	The director's film "masterpiece"
Collector of antiques	A thief	A wealthy buyer of antiques
A "strip tease" artiste	A theatrical producer	Public opinion
Aged doctor	Nurse	Nurse's sweetheart
A ship-owner	A sea captain	A storm
Thirst	A deserter from army	Military law
An aviator	Another aviator	War
A banker	Embezzling cashier	Blackmail

As usual the student will enlarge the above list as he wishes. He will endeavor to make the usual combinations and juxtapositions. It would be well for him to try combining a factor from each of Situations One and Two with one of the factors of this Situation, and see what results he may obtain. For instance, he might take "Two business men" (Persecutors in Situation One), and bring in "A poor musician" (Unfortunate in Situation Number Two) and "A stenographer" (Power in Authority in this present Situation).

What can we make out of this? Well, the two "business men" might be vaudeville agents. They know that their stenographer is in love with the poor musician. They don't want to lose her because she knows too much about their methods. So they give the poor musician a booking on a steamship going to South America, hoping the girl will forget him while he is gone.

Just after they have sent him off to the pier, their principal "meal ticket," a famous singer, enters and demands the services of the poor musician as her accompanist—otherwise she will not sing! The "two business men" race to the docks and find the boat gone! They return to the office. The famous singer has left an ultimatum. The stenographer enters with the poor musician. They have been married and the stenographer saves the situation by saying she will keep on with her job, even though wedded.

All very crude, we grant you. But we must reiterate that the examples given are devised on the spur of the moment. If we couldn't do it ourselves, how could you? If anything at all in the way of a plot can be thought out in a brief length of time, there should be real possibilities if the student will devote time and imagination to the process. We are not here to think up plots for you. It shall be our effort to strengthen and not weaken you in your studies. All we can do is point out the system and you must do the rest.

Subdivisions of the Third Situation

A (1)—THE AVENGING OF A SLAIN PARENT OR ANCESTOR

(2)—THE AVENGING OF A SLAIN CHILD OR DESCENDANT

(3)—VENGEANCE FOR A CHILD DISHONORED

(4)—THE AVENGING OF A SLAIN WIFE OR HUSBAND

(5)—VENGEANCE FOR THE DISHONOR, OR ATTEMPTED DISHONORING OF A WIFE

(6)—VENGEANCE FOR A MISTRESS SLAIN

(7)—VENGEANCE FOR A SLAIN OR INJURED FRIEND

(8)—VENGEANCE FOR A SISTER SEDUCED.

Photoplaywrights and fictionists have repeatedly used all of these phases of vengeance, many times with effectiveness and often in mere slavish imitation. An adroit, original treatment of Vengeance may produce a most impressive dramatic effect, for it is a situation that possesses virility and power.

The less melodramatic subdivisions of this Situation are:

B (1)—VENGEANCE FOR INTENTIONAL IN-
        JURY OR SPOLIATION
  (2)—VENGEANCE FOR HAVING BEEN DE-
        SPOILED DURING ABSENCE
  (3)—REVENGE FOR AN ATTEMPTED SLAY-
        ING
  (4)—REVENGE FOR A FALSE ACCUSATION
  (5)—VENGEANCE FOR VIOLATION
  (6)—VENGEANCE FOR HAVING BEEN
        ROBBED OF ONE'S OWN
  (7)—REVENGE UPON A WHOLE SEX FOR A
        DECEPTION BY ONE
C   —PROFESSIONAL PURSUIT OF CRIMI-
        NALS

The student should learn to make good use of the various Subdivisions of the Thirty-six Situations. They may readily be used in connection with the various factors suggested under the general Situation heading. Under the category of Subdivision B-7, we find the complete field of stories dealing with "woman-haters" and "man-haters"—persons who have turned against the opposite sex through being spurned by one whom they have loved deeply.

Note that Subdivision "C" is used in all mystery and detective yarns. The counterpart of this Situation will be found in the Fifth Situation, subdivision A.

One of the most interesting applications of "C" in modern writing, has been Conan Doyle's narrative of Sherlock Holmes.

"Frequently used though this Situation has been in our day, many an ancient case awaits its rejuvenescence, many a gap is yet to be filled. Indeed, among the bonds which may unite avenger and victim, more than one degree of relationship has been omitted, as well as the majority of social and business ties. The list of wrongs which might provoke reprisal is far from being exhausted, as we may assure ourselves by enumerating the kinds of offenses possible against persons or property, the varying shades of opinion of opposing parties, the different ways in which an insult may take effect, and how many and what sort of relationships may exist between Avenger and Criminal. And these questions concern merely the premises of the action.

"To this we may add all the turns and bearings, slow or instantaneous, direct or tortuous, frantic or sure, which punishment can take, the thousand resources which it offers, the points at which it may aim in its deadly course, the obstacles which chance or the defendant may present. Next introduce various secondary figures, each pursuing his own aims, as in life, inter-crossing with each other and crossing the drama—and I have sufficient esteem for the reader's capabilities to develop the subject no further." (Polti).

CHAPTER VII

FOURTH SITUATION

Vengeance Taken for Kindred Upon Kindred
(Elements: *Avenging Kinsman; Guilty Kinsman; Remembrance of the Victim, a Relative of Both*)

Famous usage of this Situation: *Hamlet* (Shakespeare)

AUGMENTING the horror of Situation Number Twenty-seven, "The Discovery of the Dishonor of One's Kindred," by the rough vigor of Situation Three, "Crime Pursued by Vengeance," the present powerful situation, which confines itself to family life, is created. It possesses as many variations as there are ties of relationship between avenger and criminal.

There are innumerable possibilities for development here, because the action of the avenger may be instigated by many different circumstances: a spontaneous desire on his own part (the simplest motive); the wish of the dying victim, or of the spirit of the dead mysteriously appearing to the living (as in *Hamlet*); an imprudent promise; a professional duty (as when the avenger is a magistrate, etc.); the necessity of saving other relatives or a beloved one or even fellow-citizens; ignorance of the kinship which exists between Avenger and Criminal.

There is also the case in which the Avenger strikes without having recognized the Criminal (for instance, in a dark room). Or, the act of intended vengeance may be but the result of an error, the supposedly guilty kinsman being found innocent, and his pseudo-executioner discovering that he has but made of himself a detestable criminal.

In considering the dynamic elements necessary in this Situation, it would seem that the third member of the triad, *Relative of Both,* would offer more attraction as a sympathetic character, a protagonist. Otherwise the results would be tragic and morbid.

The general aspect of this Situation, especially in the Subdivisions which follow later, is one of menace and gloom. And yet it can be used very effectively in comedy.

A very powerful dramatic usage of this Situation will be found in that recent stage and picture success, *The Old Maid.* In this story a girl has a child by a man who has gone to war before they have received the benefit of clergy. Her cousin had been deeply in love with this man, but when he failed to return from a trip abroad, she gave him up and married another man. Upon the death of her husband, the cousin brings the mother and child to her home, and realizing that the child can never be told of its illegitimacy, she uses this fact to avenge herself upon the mother and wins the affections of the child to herself. This naturally leads to the poignant sorrow of the mother, who is helpless to combat the situation.

In this story of *The Old Maid,* the girl-mother is the Guilty Kinsman; her cousin is the Avenging Kinsman, and the man whom they both loved serves as Remembrance of the Victim, a Relative of Both.

The student in applying the formulae listed below will need to take an imaginative viewpoint of the factors. There is a subtlety about the elements as conceived by Polti which makes a literal interpretation difficult. Remembrance of the Victim offers no active factor in the triad; therefore, we will use instead, The Victim, a Relative of Both.

AVENGING KINSMAN (*Motivating force*)	GUILTY KINS-MAN	THE VICTIM, RELATIVE OF BOTH
A husband	His brother-in-law, and business partner	His wife
A girl	Her brother, a thief	The father, a judge
A man betrothed	His fiancee	The man's mother

(Note that actual blood kinship need not be used arbitrarily. To use this Situation effectively, a close bond between the personalities may be sufficient).

A Chinese tong-leader	A white man in love with his daughter	The daughter

AVENGING KINSMAN (Motivating force)	GUILTY KINSMAN	THE VICTIM, RELATIVE OF BOTH
An honest prospector	His cousin—greedy for gold	Their uncle
A preacher	Adopted daughter	Preacher's son
A woman (social leader)	Her daughter	Her husband (lowly born)
A French apache	His sweetheart	Her father, a gendarme
Deep sea diver	His father, also a diver	Sweetheart of first
School teacher	Her father, member of School Board	Her illegitimate son
An executioner	His brother	Their mother
A mother	Her daughter	Mother's lover
A detective	His brother	Detective's sweetheart
A steel magnate	His wife	His brother
A war spy	His wife	His brother, a General

A "ticklish situation!" The student will probably have more difficulty in interpreting this Fourth Situation than in most of the others and the factors given above may not offer quite so clear a concept. This is due to the fact that The Victim, a Relative of Both the Avenging Kinsman and the Guilty Kinsman, might be forgiving towards the guilty one, an actual participant in the "crime," and made the victim, or equally revengeful against the kinsman perpetrating it for the wrong committed against him. Where the victim has been murdered, the situation resolves naturally into a case of avenger and guilty one.

We will endeavor to demonstrate the use of three of the factors. Take from the above list, "An honest prospector," "His cousin, greedy for gold," and "Their uncle." The student must dwell first upon the motivation back of each character. The honest prospector is the "avenger." Therefore, his cousin, "the guilty kinsman," must necessarily do something to wrong a kinsman of both, in order to arouse in the prospector's mind a desire for vengeance.

The honest prospector and the greedy one are out prospecting and crossing the Mojave Desert. They come across their uncle (we admit here of "coincidence"—but you will note later that the uncle is also a prospector—a sort of "family of prospectors," as it were). The uncle is dead. He died of thirst.

What can the greedy prospector do to bring about a desire for vengeance on the part of his cousin? Well, let us say that they discover a sealed envelope in one of the prospector uncle's pockets. It is addressed to the uncle's partner.

The greedy cousin wants to open it, but the honest one tells him, "It is bad luck to go against a dead man's wishes," and explains that they must deliver the letter to the uncle's partner, *unopened*.

That night, the greedy cousin opens the envelope while his honest relative is asleep. He finds inside of it a map which shows how to reach a certain cave wherein the uncle has hidden a large sum in gold nuggets.

The greedy cousin takes the mules and supplies and leaves his sleeping relative without food, water or transportation. He starts off to find the cave and succeeds.

Entering the cave he brushes against a strand of wire, which explodes a charge of dynamite. The dynamite brings down rocks and dirt across the entrance to the cave, imprisoning the guilty cousin. He frantically attempts to get out. Using his flashlight, he sees a note pinned on the wall of the cave. It is addressed to the uncle's partner and establishes that the uncle had prepared the map to lure the partner to the cave, in order that the latter would be trapped and receive vengeance for having cheated the uncle out of a large sum of money.

In other words, by opening the letter and going against his cousin's wishes, the greedy one has been caught in a trap prepared by the uncle for his dishonest partner!

Of course the story could end where the honest prospector, out for vengeance, arrives and becomes softhearted at the terrible predicament confronting his cousin. He digs the greedy cousin out in time to save his life—and thereby brings that individual back to a realization of morality and honesty.

The above makes a fairly good yarn with an "O. Henry twist." But the student will readily realize just how his imaginative powers must be called into play in order to use the factors of this Situation to evolve a story that is not too morbid and ends on a satisfying note.

Again we urge the student to enlarge the above list. He will find in the process of thinking up new factors that he will almost automatically conjure up a plot formula as he does so!

Subdivisions of the Fourth Situation

A (1)—A FATHER'S DEATH AVENGED UPON A MOTHER

  (2)—A MOTHER AVENGED UPON A FATHER

B   —A BROTHER'S DEATH AVENGED UPON A SON

C   —A FATHER'S DEATH AVENGED UPON A HUSBAND

D   —A HUSBAND'S DEATH AVENGED UPON A FATHER

It will be noted that Polti has only listed a few subdivisions. In this respect, the student must be cautioned that the subdivisions of this or any of the other situations should not be viewed as representing *all* the nuances possible within the scope of the motivation indicated by the situation title and the dynamic elements.

By carrying the relationships of the Avenger and Criminal into every possible degree, new variations will be apparent. By way of variety, the vengeance may be carried out not upon the person of the criminal himself, but upon some one dear to him. And even inanimate objects may take the place of victims.

Since the effect which the above subdivisions produce is one of horror, they should be used by the writer with a great deal of care, and in combination with other situations and subdivisions that will soften and modify the forbidding aspect.

CHAPTER VIII

FIFTH SITUATION

Pursuit

(Elements: *Punishment* and *Fugitive*)

Famous usage of this Fifth Situation: *Raffles* (Hornung)

THIS situation represents a transition into the passive of the Third and Fourth, and, in fact, of all those in which danger pursues a character. In *Pursuit,* the avenging element holds second place, or perhaps not even that; it may be, indeed, quite invisible and abstract. Our interest is held by the fugitive alone; sometimes innocent, always excusable, for the fault—if there was one—appears to have been inevitable, ordained; we do not inquire into it or blame it, which would be idle, but sympathetically suffer the consequences with our character, who, whatever he may once have been, is now but a fellow-man in danger. In the excitement of the chase, the human urge is to take the side of the person who is running away from harm. Fear of his imminent capture is sufficient to win the complete emotional sympathy of reader or audience.

Consequently, the Fifth Situation possesses a direct

and simple dramatic value. This is why it is so often used in melodrama and in slapstick comedies. In order not to trespass upon what is sadly hackneyed, the writer must combine it in new ways with other situations and develop it so that it will have a distinctive appeal.

To apply this situation to practical use without the absolute necessity of bringing in other situations, calls for the addition of *two* dynamic elements. The element, *Punishment,* is too abstract for use by the beginning writer. It would be quite possible for the more skilled craftsman to take the two elements of *Punishment* and *Fugitive,* and weave them into a powerful story, and yet it is hardly possible without bringing in another factor, maybe natural forces—such as an escaped prisoner from Devil's Island being pursued and tormented by the creatures and verdure of the jungle.

The most malleable factors to form a suitable triad in this case seems to us to be The Pursuer, The Fugitive, and The Power in Authority, which, as in former cases, lends itself so admirably to elastic definition. We will convert the elements of this situation, therefore, into such factors for plotting purposes.

THE PURSUER	THE FUGITIVE	THE POWER IN AUTHORITY
A detective	A criminal	The law
(The dynamic elements invariably used in all crime stories)		
A yacht race contestant	Another yacht race contestant	A storm

THE PURSUER	THE FUGITIVE	THE POWER IN AUTHORITY
A "war ace"	An enemy "war ace"	Courage
A killer	His victim	Sweetheart of victim
Member of a Secret Brotherhood	A traitor to the Brotherhood	A letter
The French Police	An apache	The French Foreign Legion
A bloodhound	Criminal	A sanctuary
A hurricane	A vessel	Seamanship
A blackmailer	His victim	Death
Assassins	A member of royalty	A peasant girl
A Northwest Mounted Policeman	A murderer	The elements or friends of latter
(Familiar usage in "Mountie" stories)		
A submarine	An enemy ship	Heroic sacrifice
Poverty	An unfortunate	Suicide
The G-men	A kidnapper	Person kidnapped
Disease	The victim	One who loves the victim
A hunter	An animal	Another animal
"Swing" music	A lover of classical music	Money

It will be noted that within the element Power in Authority, is also vested the factor of Punishment. Through the Power in Authority the punishment may be wrought upon either the Pursuer or the Fugitive. Under no conditions must it be assumed that the Pur-

suer is always to be the innocent party and the Fugitive
the guilty one. To make this interpretation would be
to limit the possibilities of the situation.

Offering one example of use of the above factors, we
will take "A member of a Secret Brotherhood" (Pursuer); "A traitor to the Brotherhood," (Fugitive); "A
letter" (Power in Authority).

The fugitive traitor, let us say, is a tailor. He has fled
from some foreign country, escaping from the vengeance of the Brotherhood after betraying it. He opens
a tailor shop in a small city in the United States, and
builds up a good business. Another tailor moves into
the shop next door and starts in competition with him.

The fugitive tailor is enraged until he learns that the
competitor is a member of the Brotherhood. Fearing
vengeance, and the destruction of his business, he digs a
tunnel under the building, and gets into the room of
his competitor by means of a trap door in the floor. His
competitor is working at his sewing machine. Stealthily
crossing the room, the fugitive tailor locks the door,
then turns and shoots the competitor. He places the
revolver in the dying man's hand to make it appear to
be suicide, then crawls down through the trap door,
which is hidden by a carpet, and returns via the tunnel
to his own store next door.

The police are summoned the next day by the landlord, and discover the dead body. Inasmuch as they
were forced to break down the door and the windows

are barred, they decide that it must have been suicide. While looking around, one of the officers picks up a letter which the victim had evidently written just before his death and which is addressed to his brother. Opening the letter, the officer discovers that the victim had written to his brother details concerning the traitor to the Brotherhood and prophesying that that individual would soon be giving up his store next door, knowing that he could never escape the Brotherhood's vengeance.

The police, knowing now of the enmity between the two tailors, go next door and discover the tunnel and force a confession from the guilty man, who might have committed the perfect crime were it not for the telltale letter.

This situation of *Pursuit* offers splendid possibilities for the "action" type of story. It is in its very essence *movement*. In the more literary style of story, the pursuit naturally can be of a purely psychological nature, such as, for instance, a mother's jealousy of her own daughter, due to the fact that the daughter inherits all the traits of the dead father, who had been the object of the mother's hatred before his death. The mother "pursues" her daughter psychologically, using various subtle methods to slowly but surely break the girl's will, and change her nature to one of absolute subservience.

SUBDIVISIONS OF THE FIFTH SITUATION

A—FUGITIVES FROM JUSTICE PURSUED FOR BRIGANDAGE, POLITICAL OFFENSES, ETC.

In combination with Subdivision C of Situation Three, "Professional Pursuit of Criminals," this situation forms the basis of a great many detective, crook and mystery stories. By carefully studying this type of material, the student will be able to find out the variety of ways in which it has been used.

B—PURSUED FOR A FAULT OF LOVE.
C—A HERO STRUGGLING AGAINST A POWER
D—A PSEUDO-MADMAN STRUGGLING AGAINST AN IAGO-LIKE ALIENIST.

We quote in the case of each situation and the subdivisions the words used by Polti in writing his compilation. From the above it will be noted that he defers to the classics. In many cases for the writer of modern fiction to interpret the exact meaning intended will be difficult, on that account. It is suggested, therefore, that greater stress be placed upon the application of the situation itself and its dynamic elements than in straining to find true understanding and application of the subdivisions, when they appear to be abstract and capable only of classic rendition.

CHAPTER IX

SIXTH SITUATION

Disaster

(Elements: *A Vanquished Power; a Victorious Enemy;* or *a Messenger*).

Famous usage of this situation: *The War of the Worlds* (Wells)

MANY Bible stories, much classical literature, especially the Greek epics and dramas, and most of the pages of history, are based upon this situation. It involves fear, catastrophe, the unforeseen, and it has a great, dramatic significance because it brings about the overthrowing of the powerful, and the exaltation of the weak.

In the meaning of the word "disaster," we sense a feeling of doom, of futility and sorrow. The writer should not always view this situation, however, from this morbid angle. Some of our most amusing comedies are based on this situation. For instance, a familiar comedy plot is one where the poor employee of a wealthy pompous business man turns the tables by winning the friendship of his employer's rival, and forces the employer to place him in an enviable position.

How many times this situation has been used, not alone in fiction, but in individual and national affairs! For example, it was exemplified in the defeat of Napoleon; the early conquering of England by the Romans; the disastrous attempt of the Kaiser to rule the world; in our own country, the Revolution; the vanquishing of the Indians, and so on.

Many spectacular motion pictures have been based on this situation, such as *The Birth of a Nation; Viva Villa,* and yes, even that delightful play and picture, *On Borrowed Time.*

The situation has a tendency to create powerful, dynamic themes—stories which rise above the mere love affair of two characters and which become universal in scope.

Here again, for practical, modern plotting purposes we will have to supply a third element to the triad. We believe the one most applicable to this situation would be a factor which we will entitle, "The Cause." Certainly there can be no great struggle against a "Power" without a great cause.

VANQUISHED POWER	VICTORIOUS ENEMY	THE CAUSE
A religion	Enlightenment	A leader
Floods	Human effort	Struggle for existence
A politician	Another politician	Moral issues
A racket leader	G-men	Protection
Wealthy landowner	Squatters	A woman

VANQUISHED POWER	VICTORIOUS ENEMY	THE CAUSE
A submarine	A cruiser	War
A group of fish-ermen	Another group of fishermen	Unfair practices
A cruel prison official	A prisoner	Official's daughter
Owner of a factory	His employees	Disease
A banker	A lawyer	Legal technicalities
A husband	His wife's lover	The wife
A stock manipulator	A stockholder	Justice
A man	A girl	Love
Disease	Science	Death
A cattle rustler	A cow-puncher	A girl
A mob	A sheriff	A criminal
Popular opinion	An artist	Artist's paintings
Love	Hatred	Dishonesty

It will be seen that most elements which can be applied under this situation are more or less abstract and nebulous. In many cases this is due to the thematic value of the situation. It does not, therefore, offer such clear-cut factors as some of the others. It necessitates more thought and application on the part of the writer. The human element must be brought into play using the situation as an underlying idea, rather than using the situation as a plot basis and building from the human element towards a theme.

Take, for instance, the factors given above of "A submarine" (Vanquished Power); "A cruiser" (Victorious Enemy); "War" (The Cause). We have no personalities here until we build them into the story. We know that there is a battle between a cruiser and a submarine, brought about on account of war between the nations designated by the ensigns on each vessel. But the mere recounting of a battle between the cruiser and the submarine, while it might make good newspaper headlines and reading, would hardly hold the attention of the reader of fiction, throughout several thousands of words, without personalities being involved.

Therefore, to use such factors for entertaining reading, it would probably have to resolve itself into intense interest in the *individuals* serving as captains of the rival vessels. For example, the captain of the cruiser might be the brother-in-law of the captain of the submarine. In destroying the submarine, he realizes that he may also be destroying his love life. The reader is then interested in the battle, because it has a powerful human problem involved and not merely a matter of war tactics between seamen who are no more than that to the reader.

In some of the situations it is more in the nebulous power of the struggle that inspiration will be found than in searching for concrete plot elements.

Subdivisions of the Sixth Situation:

A (1)—DEFEAT SUFFERED
    (2)—A FATHERLAND DESTROYED

(3)—THE FALL OF HUMANITY

(4)—A NATURAL CATASTROPHE

B   —A MONARCH OVERTHROWN

C (1)—INGRATITUDE SUFFERED

"Of all the blows of misfortune, this (C-1) is perhaps the most poignant." (Polti)

(2)—THE SUFFERING OF UNJUST PUNISHMENT OR ENMITY

(3)—AN OUTRAGE SUFFERED

D (1)—ABANDONMENT BY A LOVER OR A HUSBAND

(2)—CHILDREN LOST BY THEIR PARENTS

The last mentioned subdivisions should not be used indiscriminately, because they have been well nigh exhausted in the photoplay as well as in stage drama. They should only be incorporated in a plot when they are absolutely essential, and form a logical part of the story development.

It will be noted that we list in most cases the subdivisions *after* discussion of the situation and its basic elements. This is done so that the student will have an understanding of the principles involved in the situation before endeavoring to apply the subdivisions. The student, may, however, find it easier to read the entire chapter first, including the subdivisions, and then go back to the beginning before making practical applications of the elements.

Chapter X

SEVENTH SITUATION

Falling Prey to Cruelty or Misfortune

(Elements: *An Unfortunate; a Master or a Misfortune*)

Famous usage of this Situation: *Jane Eyre* (Charlotte Bronte)

IN THIS situation, the central, "sympathetic" character is placed in a seemingly hopeless predicament. Consequently, a strong appeal may be made to the sympathy of the reader or spectator. While there is here a wealth of excellent dramatic material, much care must be exercised in selecting forms of cruelty and misfortune that will convince the reader of their reality. Exaggeration will reduce pathos to bathos, and drama of high seriousness to burlesque. But, on the other hand, the cruelty or misfortune should be great enough to be of real emotional interest.

To keep this situation from becoming starkly tragic, and to use it to advantage for stories of the popular type, as well as for pictures and radio, it seems necessary to bring in an element which will serve to soften the misfortune or save the Unfortunate from dire distress. For the stage, it might be used in its present form, for the theater allows more morbid presentations.

We will, therefore, in our list of factors, use the following headings:

AN UNFORTU-NATE	THE INSTIGA-TOR OR CAUSE OF THE MISFOR-TUNE	A SAVIOR
A man in love	The girl he loves	Another girl
A murderer	Circumstantial evidence	The guilty
A baseball player	A rival player	A girl
A policeman	A crook	Crook's sweetheart
A refugee	Racial hatred	A friend
A wife	A man in love with her	Her mother
A farmer	Drouth	Rain
An inmate of an insane asylum	His brother	A fire
A released convict	Liberty	A philanthropist
A thief	Poverty	Victim of theft
A preacher	Tolerance	A dream
A deserter	His sweetheart	Heroism
A beachcomber	A criminal act	A native girl
A native youth	Education	Disease
A lighthouse keeper	A storm	Coast Guard
A miner	Disaster	The Bible
An artist	Wealth	Poverty

It seems timely here to again urge the student to work out combinations of elements, blending the factors of different situations. For example: Take "A treasure hunter" (Pursuer in the Fifth Situation); "A girl," (Victorious Enemy in the Sixth Situation,) and "A refugee," (Unfortunate One in this present situation). Many thoughts immediately come to mind in dwelling on this rather peculiar combination. We have a treasure hunter seeking or "pursuing" a treasure in pearls, hidden, let us say, by the father of the girl (Victorious Enemy). The girl is victorious inasmuch as she reaches the treasure first. Naturally, she is the enemy of the treasure hunter, as he has endeavored to cheat her out of her lawful inheritance.

On the island where the treasure is found by the girl is a "refugee." At one time he was a famous actor but ruined through a serious scandal. Unable to face the world, he came to the island to live as a recluse. The girl falls in love with him and is informed of his true identity by the treasure hunter. It turns out that the refugee was the cause of her own mother's suicide. The treasure is the price the refugee offered as recompense to the girl's father. The father spurned it then, but later, on his death bed, revealed its whereabouts through a map, in order that his daughter might not face poverty. The refugee confesses to the accusation; the girl throws the treasure into the sea, and departs, utterly disillusioned.

The above illustrates a rather far fetched story outline, but it demonstrates the intricacies possible through a combination of various factors, and most certainly is conducible to exercise of the imagination. Such exercise is of the utmost importance to the student, regardless of whether or not immediate results are satisfactory. It might be well, in fact, for the writer to let his imagination "run loose," then bring it under control through rearrangement of the plot threads and by molding and remolding of material.

We believe that such exercises of the imagination will, in time, give the student sufficient training so that he can conjure up in his own mind plot ideas and formulae which will have much more consistency and realism and be of proper literary value.

Subdivisions of the Seventh Situation:

A   —THE INNOCENT MADE THE VICTIM OF AMBITIOUS INTRIGUE

B   —THE INNOCENT DESPOILED BY THOSE WHO SHOULD PROTECT

C (1)—THE POWERFUL DISPOSSESSED AND WRETCHED

(2)—A FAVORITE OR AN INTIMATE FINDS HIMSELF FORGOTTEN

D   —THE UNFORTUNATE ROBBED OF THEIR ONLY HOPE

For the most part, the history of the world is that of persecution and suffering. The presentation of such suffering is of dramatic value to the degree to which the writer can awaken the sympathy of the reader. While the various phases of this situation have been used over and over, its scope is so great that there are still infinite possibilities for development.

CHAPTER XI

EIGHTH SITUATION

Revolt

(Elements: *Tyrant* and *Conspirator*)

Famous usage of this Situation: *A Doll's House* (Ibsen)

MUCH of the best modern fiction and drama is concerned with *revolt,* either of an individual, or of many. There is, for instance, Galsworthy's play, *The Mob,* where a single man opposes an entire populace, Shaw's *Fanny's First Play,* etc.

In the short story, the revolt of one individual who influences others is of more value than that of many, for it leads to a greater concentration and dramatic tension.

In history, we have many examples of mass revolt, i.e., the French Revolution; the overthrow of the Czar; our own American Revolution, and many other events wherein the oppressed destroy tyrannical powers.

In writing, *revolt* is apt to be construed in an epic way, and its usage disregarded because of the difficulty in presentation. As a matter of fact, revolt of the individual represents one of our most commonplace aspects of life. Human beings continually revolt against poverty, disease, political oppression and the like. In domestic life, the wife will revolt against the small tyrannies of her husband or children, and vice versa. The situation is, therefore, quite tremendous in its scope, and of the utmost value in drama, tragedy and comedy.

In order to form a triad for plotting purposes, it is again necessary to create an element, which was inferred by Polti, but not stated. In this case, we believe the third element should be "The Cause,"—or the reason for the conspiracy. This gives us the following:

TYRANT	CONSPIRATOR	THE CAUSE
A king	The people	Unjust taxation
	(A familiar historic basis for uprisings)	
Two wives	Their husbands	Their children
A girl	Her father	Her sweetheart
A politician	His opponent	Dishonesty
A gangster	Rival gangster	Power
White ruler of native colony	The natives	Oppression
An atheist	A believer (girl)	Love
A criminal	A girl	Revenge
A picture producer	Rival producer	Monopoly
A miser	His children	His wife
An actress	Her sweetheart	Jealousy
Leader of narcotic ring	The police	The law

TYRANT	CONSPIRATOR	THE CAUSE
Disease	Science	An epidemic
A dancer	A rajah	Passion
A rajah	A dancer	Impoverished kindred

(Using reversal of some of the factors)

A cattle rustler	A cow boy	A girl

(Familiar "Western" formula)

A construction engineer	Greed	A woman

(Note that a human emotion forms the conspiring element in the above. Greed for gold to please a woman conspires against the better nature of the engineer)

Captain of a Whaler	His crew	Injustice

(Mutiny on the high seas comes aptly within the scope of this situation)

A factory owner	His employes	A rival factory owner

The ramifications possible under this heading of *Revolt* are endless. The element of "heart interest" can be brought into play here to the utmost advantage. A predominant human trait is to witness the downfall of a tyrant with pleasure; to sympathize with the underdog, and his plans to destroy the perpetrator of injustices. Withal, it is a deeply poignant situation and essentially powerful and dramatic.

Subdivisions of the Eighth Situation:

A (1)—A CONSPIRACY CHIEFLY OF ONE IN-
DIVIDUAL
(2)—A CONSPIRACY OF SEVERAL

The most frequent use of these subdivisions has been in mystery and "crook" stories, and various types of propaganda plays. They are valuable in that they allow for the building up of mystery and intrigue, and for the creating and maintaining of intense suspense.

B (1)—REVOLT OF ONE INDIVIDUAL, WHO
INFLUENCES AND INVOLVES OTHERS
(2)—A REVOLT OF MANY

CHAPTER XII

NINTH SITUATION

Daring Enterprise

(Elements: *A Bold Leader; an Object; an Adversary*)
Famous usage of this Situation: *Around the World in Eighty Days* (Jules Verne)

"THE Conflict, which forms the framework of all dramatic situations, is, in the Ninth, clearly drawn, undisguised. A clever plan, a bold attempt, sangfroid,—and victory!" (*Polti*)

Situation Nine has scarcely been touched by modern drama. It is especially suitable for the screen. Its infinite variations—depending upon the characters, the object sought, the many kinds of difficulties that could interfere with the Leader's success—have received little attention from the dramatist. In stories and books, it has obviously been used in many, many variations. But its possibilities are infinite.

Under this situation, as will be shown later in our list of the subdivisions, comes that grim spectre, "War." Within the scope of this situation, therefore, lies the

most powerful evil influence against which mankind
has to contend.

Here indeed is a situation which the student can
use to the utmost advantage and it is especially useful
in combination with other situations.

Encompass the whole field of adventure and you
will find that the elements of this situation govern,—
a Bold Leader, an Objective, an Adversary! It probably
represents one of the most virile of all the situations.
Abraham Lincoln, Daniel Boone, Christopher Colum-
bus, Napoleon, Caesar,—countless names which are em-
blazoned across the pages of world history,—each
reached the pinnacle of his success through daring
enterprise, whether that enterprise fell within the category of mental or physical conflict.

Even in the realm of the fairy story, this situation
has been used many, many times. It has been used in
allegories, epic poems, mythologies; it is the high light
of great biographies. Yes, even the Bible tells of daring
enterprise; what more striking example could be found
than in the defeat of Goliath by David?

We tabulate a list of factors under this dynamic situation:

A BOLD LEADER	AN OBJECTIVE	AN ADVERSARY
A dictator	Needed territory	A nation
(The basis of our present European war)		
An explorer	Exotic plants	Natural barriers

A BOLD LEADER	*AN OBJECTIVE*	*AN ADVERSARY*
A prize-fighter	Championship	A rival
A labor leader	Better working conditions	A factory owner
A revolutionist	Power	A rival party
A crook	Wealth	The law
A Chinese bandit leader	White woman	Her fiance
Northwest Mounted Policeman	A criminal	Another criminal
An author	A new economic system	Public opinion
An aviator	A fortification	An enemy aviator
A newspaper editor	"Racket busting"	Leader of racket
A treasure hunter	The treasure	Savages
A hypnotist	Supremacy	A murderer
A scientist	A "death ray"	A preacher
A mayor	Clean government	A political power
An adventurer	Martian exploration	Martians

(A "fantastic" story formula)

Pilot of seaplane	A rescue	The elements
A bandit leader	Money	A sheriff

The student might justly ask how a suspenseful story could develop out of such elements as "Pilot of seaplane," "A rescue," and "The elements," contending that the factor "The elements" offers no human equation,—no antagonistic force upon which to base a conflict. A little thought to the matter and a review of some of our outstanding short stories will reveal how aptly natural forces can be used effectively. In this case, we are, of course, supposing that the pilot of the seaplane is carrying serum to the members of a freighter crew, the ship having run aground on a far Northern shore. In the pilot's fight to bring the plane to the designated place when confronted by wind, rain, blizzards, mist, dense clouds, etc., as much tension can be attained as if the pilot were endeavoring to carry on to his destination in the realization that his co-pilot has suddenly gone mad. It all depends on how the story is written, and, true, it does require a masterly touch. On this account, the student is urged, in his beginning work, to adhere closely to the human element in completing the trinity.

In this situation, the Object, or Objective, may likely be an individual ambition, an inanimate object or objects, such as gold coins, furs, antiquities, fossils, etc., or a cause. This leaves a lack of the human element among the factors, especially if combined with a like factor for the Adversary. (For example: An author; a new economic system; public opinion.) In such cases, additional characters must be brought into the story to personify such rather nebulous elements. In the above case of "The author, etc.," the author's secretary, who is in love with him, is his staunch supporter, and public opinion may largely be guided by one certain individual, who is bitterly opposed to the author's scheme.

To attack such factors in any other way would probably result in pure narrative or an "article" rather than a story.

Subdivisions of the Ninth Situation:

A   —PREPARATIONS FOR WAR
B (1)—WAR
   (2)—A COMBAT
C (1)—CARRYING OFF A DESIRED PERSON
       OR OBJECT
   (2)—RECAPTURE OF A DESIRED OBJECT
   (3)—ADVENTUROUS EXPEDITIONS
   (4)—ADVENTURE UNDERTAKEN FOR THE
       PURPOSE OF OBTAINING A BELOVED
       WOMAN

These subdivisions form the basis of nearly all fairy tales, a great deal of romance, and the so-called "adventure" stories of today. Being capable of infinite and varied development, they offer the observing and wide-awake writer excellent suggestions for stories.

"The Ninth Situation thus summarizes the poetry of war, of robbery, of surprise, of desperate chance,—the poetry of the clear-eyed adventurer, of man beyond the restraints of artificial civilizations, of Man in the original acceptance of the term. . . ." (*Polti*)

Chapter XIII

TENTH SITUATION

Abduction

(Elements: *The Abductor; the Abducted; the Guardian*) .

Famous usage of this Situation: *Trilby* (Du Maurier)

OF THE Thirty-six Situations this one is perhaps the most exhausted, for probably no other has been so frequently used. It is found usually in melodramas. It has not been employed so frequently in sound dramatic plots, and this phase of it offers the writer excellent opportunity to build up vital and appealing stories.

This especially applies in reference to one of the later listed subdivisions, *Rescue of a Soul in Captivity to Error*. Although apparently more suited to religious or morality stories, it could also be intended to include the redemption of a criminal, persuasion against suicide, or guidance to a higher life of anyone living in sin or seeking vengeance, and so on.

The first thought that comes to mind in regard to this situation is, of course, the kidnaping of a child.

It is almost futile to attempt to use the situation in this trite fashion. Abduction of a woman has been used so many times in Western and adventure stories that the idea requires the most unusual treatment to give it novelty.

As a whole, the situation must be dealt with very cagily by the student, or he will be apt to follow well-trodden paths.

Some of the factors given below are conventional, but they must be listed as vitally applicable to the situation.

THE ABDUCTOR	THE ABDUCTED	THE GUARDIAN (Or reason for abduction)
A kidnaper	A child	The parents (Motive: money)
(The most familiar formula)		
A man	A woman	Her lover or husband (Motive: passion)
A mother	Her child	The father (Motive: love)
A gangster	A detective	The law
A man	His brother	Love of an evil woman (Motive)
A judge	A criminal	Salvation (Motive)
An astronomer	Another astronomer	A new heavenly concept (Motive)

THE ABDUCTOR	THE ABDUCTED	THE GUARDIAN (*Or reason for abduction*)
A cattle rustler	Rancher's daughter	Cow-puncher in love with her (Guardian)
(Familiar Western formula)		
A puritanical father	His son	The frivolous mother
An Arab sheik	A girl	Girl's lover or family (Guardian) (Motive: passion)
(Old "Rudolph Valentino" story formula)		
Leader of cult	A group of people (Mental abduction)	Wealth (Motive)
A politician	Another politician	Revenge
A girl	Man she loves	His wife (Guardian)
Member of royalty	A girl	Man in love with her
A play producer	An actress	A playwright
A man	A dog	Dog's owner
A preacher	A girl	Proprietor of house of prostitution

The factors of this situation can be aptly combined with factors of other situations and it is advisable to make such combinations in an effort to achieve novelty of treatment.

Subdivisions of the Tenth Situation:

A   —ABDUCTION OF AN UNWILLING
        WOMAN
B   —ABDUCTION OF A CONSENTING
        WOMAN
C (1)—RECAPTURE OF THE WOMAN WITH-
        OUT THE SLAYING OF THE ABDUC-
        TOR
   (2)—THE SAME CASE, WITH THE SLAYING
        OF THE RAVISHER
D (1)—RESCUE OF A CAPTIVE FRIEND
   (2)—OF A CHILD
   (3)—OF A SOUL IN CAPTIVITY TO ERROR

Infinite variations of this last subdivision are possible, and it can be used very effectively. Perhaps the most outstanding motion picture based on *Rescue of a Soul in Captivity to Error,* was that old, yet never-to-be-forgotten production of *The Miracle Man.*

To the alert creative mind that can endow Situation Ten with novel development, it still offers interesting possibilities.

CHAPTER XIV

ELEVENTH SITUATION

The Enigma

(Elements: *Interrogator; Seeker;* and *Problem*)

Famous usage of this Situation: *Adventures of Sherlock Holmes* (Conan Doyle)

THIS situation is of histrionic value, because it is one of the best situations for creating and sustaining suspense. Its principal usage on the screen has been in "crook" plays and in mystery stories. It has many other possibilities for that medium as well as in fiction.

"This situation possesses theatrical interest par excellence, since the spectator, his curiosity aroused by the problem, easily becomes so absorbed as to fancy it is himself who is actually solving it. A combat of the intelligence with opposing wills, the Eleventh Situation may be fitly symbolized by an interrogation point." (*Polti*)

When we speak of "enigma" in plotting, we almost invariably think of the detective-mystery story. This type of yarn is generally a blending of this situation with the Fifth Situation, *Pursuit.* However, it has much more subtle usages. It applies to scientists seeking greater knowledge of natural resources, chemical formulae, serums and anti-toxins, etc. It applies to the metaphysician, in his probing for the essential nature of reality, or the preternatural or supernatural. The teacher is a living symbol of "interrogator". We are all "seekers" and we all have "problems." The depth of thought, therefore, to which one can go, in dwelling upon this situation of *The Enigma* is incalculable.

The elements are rather subtle and in practical usage must be given broad delineation. This should be kept in mind by the student in his study of the following factors and in their application; also, in his task of adding to the list.

INTERROGA-TOR (Or interested party)	SEEKER	PROBLEM (Or object or Person sought)
A detective	The law	A crime
	(Detective-mystery formula)	
A man in love	The girl he loves	Financial security
A father	His son	A career
An employer	An employee	Money
Head of a found-ling home	A mother	Her child
A peasant	A king	Public welfare
A health inspector	A tenant	Better housing
A lawyer	A client	Divorce

INTERROGA-TOR (Or interested party)	SEEKER	PROBLEM (Or object or Person sought)
A criminal	A stamp collector	A rare stamp
Greed	A man	Love
(The psychological conflict in a man's mind of "money versus love.")		
An explorer	His financial backer	Rare animals, plants or relics
A native girl	A deep sea diver	Pearls
Foreman of a jury	A murderer	Moral issues
(Largely the juror's mental conflict or "self-interrogation.")		
A miser	A suppliant	Money
A woman	A man	Passion
A co-respondent (woman)	The wife	The husband
An art connoisseur	An art collector	Work of art

In our modern conception of the word "situation," as related to story plotting, some of the Polti situations seem to fall within the definition of "theme," if the word *theme* is interpreted to mean "the abstract essence of a story." The elements of Interrogator, Seeker, and Problem, combining to solve an "enigma," present no clean-cut basis for a plot situation. In many of the situations it will be noted that there is a lack of well-defined elements so necessary to modern story plotting.

For classical presentation and for beautiful narrative, there is no question of their adequacy, but for practical

usage, especially in the writing of the screen play or
stage play, many of the situations can only be used as
a basis for liberal interpretation. Herein lies our difficulty. So many interpretations might be given to them
that it is hard to choose the one most likely to be of
greatest assistance to the plot builder. It is therefore
suggested that the student refrain from adhering too
closely to the interpretations given herein, but to find
one which might allow him more elasticity, according
to his own particular viewpoint.

Subdivisions of the Eleventh Situation:

A   —SEARCH FOR A PERSON WHO MUST
        BE FOUND ON PAIN OF DEATH

B (1)—A RIDDLE TO BE SOLVED ON PAIN OF
        DEATH

   (2)—THE SAME CASE, IN WHICH THE
        RIDDLE IS PROPOSED BY THE COV-
        ETED WOMAN

C (1)—TEMPTATIONS OFFERED WITH THE
        OBJECT OF DISCOVERING HIS NAME

   (2)—TEMPTATIONS OFFERED WITH THE
        OBJECT OF ASCERTAINING THE SEX

   (3)—TESTS FOR THE PURPOSE OF ASCER-
        TAINING THE MENTAL CONDITION

Chapter XV

TWELFTH SITUATION

Obtaining

(Elements: *A Solicitor* and *an Adversary Who is Refusing;* or *an Arbitrator* and *Opposing Parties*).

Famous usage of this situation: *Tutt and Mr. Tutt* (Arthur Train)

"Diplomacy and eloquence here come into play. An end is to be obtained, an object to be gained. What interests may not be put at stake, what weighty arguments or influences removed, what intermediaries or disguises may be used to transform anger into benevolence, rancor into renouncement; to put the Despoiler in the place of the Despoiled? What mines may be sprung, what counter-mines discovered!—what unexpected revolts of submissive instruments! This dialectic contest which arises between reason and passion, sometimes subtle and persuasive, sometimes forceful and violent, provides a fine situation, as natural as it is original." (*Polti*)

Obviously, this situation is of more use on the stage

and in pictures than in fiction. The appeal is in the eloquence of the Solicitor or Arbitrator, and implies verbal expression. A recent example of its application will be found in the recent stage play, *One-Third of a Nation,* wherein an eloquent plea is made for proper housing.

Although this situation is used in some degree in the majority of stories, for instance, even where the man pleads with the girl for her hand in marriage,—in the meaning which Polti has given to it, it probably has been the basis for the smallest number of stories of any of the situations, if we make an exception of the Subdivision, "Efforts to obtain an object by ruse or force." (Listed later.)

The true meaning of the situation (or *theme,* in this case) is that whereby an object or purpose is achieved almost entirely through the persuasive powers of the Solicitor, his logic, eloquence of speech, understanding of the issue, etc. Substantially, it is not so dramatic possibly as most of the other situations. There is a certain element of "trickery" involved, an emphasis on *cleverness,* rather than on deeply rooted human traits.

So many of the situations apply to the momentous happenings in real life that it is difficult at times even to apply them to fiction. This situation, for instance, is so applicable to the eloquence of political spokesmen, to advocates in courts of law, to labor leaders haranguing their followers, that its use implies a realistic, rather than an imaginary course of events.

It will readily be seen that a readjustment of the dynamic elements of this situation will have to be made in order to apply it to advantage in plot building.

In this case, let us disregard the triad and bring in *four* factors. This seems necessary to handle the situation effectively.

A SOLICI-TOR	AN AD-VERSARY	OBJECT OR REASON FOR SOLIC-ITATION	ARBITRA-TOR
A lawyer	Opposing lawyer	A case at law	Judge
(The most familiar usage of this situation)			
A politician	His opponent	An office	The public
(The situation applied to every-day political rivalries)			
A man	Father of his sweetheart	Girl's hand in marriage	Girl's mother
The accused	Prosecuting attorney	Justice	A jury
An employee	His employer	Employer's daughter	The daughter
A labor leader	Factory owner	Welfare of employes	A purchaser of goods
A sheriff	A mob	A criminal	Mob leader
An ambassador	A ruler	International issues	Ambassador's wife
A soldier	A prosecutor	Pardon for a crime	A Judge-Advocate

A SOLICI- TOR	AN AD- VERSARY	OBJECT OR REASON FOR SOLIC- ITATION	ARBITRA- TOR
A mutinous sailor	A sea captain	Treasure	Power (Man- power or will-power)
An actress	Another ac- tress	A role	A producer
An old man	Death	Life	Love
	(Formula of *"On Borrowed Time"*)		
A general	A ruler	Human life	Ruler's wife
A girl	A police offi- cer	Girl's lover	Duty (Men- tal with offi- cer)

This situation, maybe as much as or more than any of the others, requires a blending with other situations. Many of the above combinations of factors represent trite formulae, and yet it would be difficult to arrange the factors to better advantage. However, to combine the factor of *Solicitor,* especially, with other situations may lead to original and unusual plots.

Let us take a combination at random,—An explorer, (Situation Nine—A Bold Leader); an actress (Situation Ten—The Abducted); an artist (Situation Six— Victorious Enemy) and lastly, a general (the Solicitor in this present situation. In this case we are combining four elements.

Rather bewildering, isn't it? Let us see what kind

of plot could be worked out of such a jumble of characters, all with such widely different motives. Well, it seems impossible to us to consider these elements even momentarily, without getting some ideas. We trust that this will apply in the case of the writer studying the situations as a stimulant to his imagination.

The explorer, or Bold Leader, is, of course, in love with the actress. And so is the artist. The artist, however, has definitely won the girl's affections. Unable to give her up, the explorer abducts her as he is leaving on an exploration trip to South America. The girl, being modern and sensible, makes the best of the situation, although definitely repulsing the explorer's advances. The artist, enraged, starts in pursuit of the explorer and the girl.

The next scene will take place in a small country in South America. The general (Solicitor) is trying to take over the government for himself and his party, which is strictly militaristic. He is defeated and forced to flee. In his escape, he is befriended by the artist, who has just arrived in the country. The artist takes the general into his confidence. In return for what the artist has done for him, the general gets together a few of his soldiers and boards the explorer's boat, which is lying in the harbor.

With great eloquence the general convinces the explorer that if he can obtain the "loan" of the actress, he can put over with the people that she is a wealthy

American heiress willing to invest money in developing the country, and thus win the opposition over to himself and his faction.

Finally persuaded, and the actress "sold" on the plan, which she feels will show her histrionic ability to great advantage, the explorer gives in. The general goes ashore with the girl, who is also anxious to get out of the clutches of her abductor, the explorer. The general turns her over to the waiting artist, and there is a big clinch between the two, with a happy ending for all save the noble general, who bravely walks away to face the guns of his enemies.

Subdivisions of the Twelfth Situation:

A—EFFORTS TO OBTAIN AN OBJECT BY RUSE OR FORCE

B—ENDEAVOR BY MEANS OF PERSUASIVE ELOQUENCE ALONE

C—ELOQUENCE WITH AN ARBITRATOR

Situation Twelve bears a direct relation to Situations One and Eleven, *Supplication,* and *Deliverance.* It was used commonly in classical drama, where the spoken word carried such impressive dramatic value. Subdivision A figures extensively in obvious, melodramatic stories. But the more subtle phases of the situation have been by no means exhausted.

CHAPTER XVI

THIRTEENTH SITUATION

Enmity of Kinsmen

(Elements: *A Malevolent Kinsman; a Hated or Reciprocally Hating Kinsman.*)

Famous usage of this Situation: *Cain* (Byron)

THIS situation is a good example of dramatic contrast. It might be stated, "hatred of one who should be loved," and is therefore the reverse of Situation Fourteen, "love of one who should be hated." The more closely are drawn the bonds of hatred between the kinsmen at enmity, the more savage and dangerous their outbursts of hate are rendered. When the hatred is mutual, it will better characterize this situation than when it exists on one side only, in which case one of the relatives becomes Tyrant, and the other Victim, the ensemble resulting in Situations Five, Eight, Thirty, etc. It is difficult, however, to use this situation convincingly, because there are so few elements of discord powerful enough to cause the breaking of the strongest human ties.

While this situation has, obviously, great dramatic value which may be turned to good account in stories and plays, the chief danger in using it lies in its tendency toward exaggerated and unconvincing melodrama. The student should use it only when it arises in a plot with seeming inevitability, so that it will "ring true."

In order to form a dramatic trinity we will use the following factors:

A MALEVO-LENT KINSMAN	A HATED KINS-MAN	THE CAUSE
A mother-in-law	A son-in-law	The daughter (wife)
(Famous "mother-in-law" situation)		
A father	A son	The mother
An uncle	A nephew	A woman
Man of wealth	His impoverished brother	Impoverished brother's peace of mind
A dictator	His brother	Politics
A criminal	His uncle, a Prosecutor	Fear
A jeweler	His cousin	Murder of a loved one
Chinese politician	His daughter	Her marriage to a white man
A banker	His son-in-law	Banker's daughter
A banker's daughter	Her sister-in-law	Daughter's lover
A husband	His wife's former husband	Jealousy

A MALEVO-LENT KINSMAN	*A HATED KINS-MAN*	*THE CAUSE*
A mistress	Her paramour	Paramour's wife
A king	His brother	A throne
A wife	Her husband	Her daughter by first marriage
A smuggler	His brother, a Coast Guard official	Adherence of brother to duty
An aunt	Her niece	Wealth
A man	His half-brother	A pledge broken
A woman	Adopted daughter	Woman's lover
Adopted daughter	Her foster-mother	Murder
A girl	Her sister	A career

The list of possible conflicts between kindred might be extended for pages. And yet, individually or collectively, the result is the same—somewhat disagreeable formulae. A struggle ensuing between relatives unless attacked with a humorous touch, is very apt to be depressing, inasmuch as it tends to destroy cherished family solidarity.

If the student will endeavor to recall stories, plays or pictures based on this situation, he may very likely find his mind a blank. In the classics, the situation was used extensively and even attained distinction. But aside from numerous "feud" stories, the conflict between relatives during the Civil War and to a lesser extent during the Revolution, the situation has attained no outstanding honors that we can recall insofar as American literature is concerned.

Considering the above, it would be well for the student to use this situation almost invariably in combination with other situations, unless, as stated, it is used as a comedy formula. Many amusing comedies have been written showing the conflict between a husband and his brother-in-law, an aunt and her nephew, or an uncle and his nephew. *Charley's Aunt*, famous old stage play, is based on this situation as treated from a humorous standpoint.

Subdivisions of the Thirteenth Situation:

A   —HATRED OF BROTHERS
  (1)—ONE BROTHER HATED BY SEVERAL
  (2)—RECIPROCAL HATRED
  (3)—HATRED BETWEEN RELATIVES FOR REASONS OF SELF-INTEREST

B   —HATRED OF FATHER AND SON
  (1)—OF THE SON FOR THE FATHER
  (2)—MUTUAL HATRED
  (3)—HATRED OF DAUGHTER FOR FATHER

C   —HATRED OF GRANDFATHER FOR GRANDSON

D   —HATRED OF FATHER-IN-LAW FOR SON-IN-LAW

E   —HATRED OF MOTHER-IN-LAW FOR DAUGHTER-IN-LAW

F   —INFANTICIDE

Chapter XVII

FOURTEENTH SITUATION

Rivalry of Kinsmen

(Elements: *The Preferred Kinsman; the Rejected Kinsman; the Object.*)

Famous usage of this Situation: *The Man in the Iron Mask* (Dumas)

THIS situation occurs frequently both in fiction and on the stage and screen. The most obvious form in which it appears in screen stories is the rivalry between the good and the bad brother both in love with the same girl, the nobility of one contrasting with the villainy of the other. There is a great deal of strength and vitality in this situation, but, as in the preceding one, there is a very real danger of exaggeration and implausibility.

Because there are innumerable phases of rivalry between kinsmen that have not been exploited by the modern writer, this situation offers excellent material to the creative imagination. If the situation is thoroughly *humanized,* instead of being treated in a sensational way, it may be developed in a subtle and interesting fashion.

The poignancy of its appeal will depend upon the fineness of the characterization. For example, if the rivalry between two girls of quite opposite temperament and character, cousins, is combined with the sacrifice of one for the other, resulting in a deep, human drama that grips at the heart, it very likely would win the complete sympathy of the reader or an audience.

PREFERRED KINSMAN	REJECTED KINSMAN	OBJECT (Or Reason of Rivalry)
A lawyer	His brother	A girl
A circus girl	Her sister	A lion trainer
A brewer	His son	Unmarried woman
A salesman	His son	Married woman
Wealthy woman	Her daughter	Daughter's step-father
A poet	His cousin, a radio station owner	A radio program
A dancer	Her cousin, a dance director	Fame
A rancher	His best friend, a banker	Ranch property

(Kinship includes "friendship" according to Polti's interpretation)

A prize-fighter	His brother, a prize-fighter	The championship
A radio operator	His friend, a sea-captain	A girl

PREFERRED KINSMAN	REJECTED KINSMAN	OBJECT (Or Reason of Rivalry)
A spy	His wife	Army secrets or plans
A wife	Her husband	Husband's brother
A bandit	His brother, a detective	Brother's sweetheart
A burlesque queen	Her husband, a newspaper man	Their child
A prince	His mother (fairy queen)	A witch
	(Fairy story formula)	
Captain of Chinese pirate ship	His brother, a government official	A dancer (girl)
A native chief	His sweetheart	A white man
A deep-sea diver	Another diver (friends)	Treasure lost by a girl
A politician	His father, a labor leader	Political issues
A vaudeville actor	His wife, an actress	A career
A daughter	Her mother	The father

Aside from rivalry of kindred, the theme carries tremendous scope. Commercialism today is based on rivalry between corporations, factories, shops, job-hunters, office employes, etc. It is intriguing from the standpoint of fiction. Nearly everyone enjoys a tense struggle between individuals to attain some desired objective. Nearly all "sport" stories are based on this situation, *Rivalry*. Race-track stories, prize-fight stories and ski-jumping yarns generally resolve themselves into a keen rivalry between the factions involved. If the rivalry is portrayed interestingly, the reader or spectator is in a state of tension, awaiting the outcome and "pulling" for the one he wants to win.

As a general rule stories based on rivalry are somewhat naive, and play much more upon the emotions than the intellect. And yet, the mental phase of rivalry between two astute opponents, such as two scientists, two attorneys, two political strategists, may carry with it real suspense and intense interest.

The student may dwell upon this situation to his advantage and find in it much that is unusual and refreshing.

Subdivisions of the Fourteenth Situation:

A (1)—MALICIOUS RIVALRY OF A BROTHER
  (2)—MALICIOUS RIVALRY OF TWO BROTHERS
  (3)—RIVALRY OF TWO BROTHERS WITH ADULTERY ON THE PART OF ONE
  (4)—RIVALRY OF SISTERS
B (1)—RIVALRY OF FATHER AND SON FOR AN UNMARRIED WOMAN
  (2)—RIVALRY OF FATHER AND SON FOR A MARRIED WOMAN
  (3)—CASE SIMILAR TO THE TWO FOREGOING, BUT IN WHICH THE OBJECT

IS ALREADY THE WIFE OF THE FATHER

(4)—RIVALRY OF MOTHER AND DAUGHTER

C —RIVALRY OF COUSINS

D —RIVALRY OF FRIENDS

We will give a few examples of plot ideas based on some of the above subdivisions:

(1)—A woman attains recognition as leader of a fight against social disease. Her jealous sister, a nonentity, confronts her with the revelation that their own brother has acquired a social disease.

(2)—A successful actress finds herself relegated to the background through the achievements of her own daughter.

(3)—A man accomplishes an heroic deed to save the life of the girl he loves, to find that his brother's intellectual superiority outweighs his physical prowess in the girl's affections.

(4)—A fanatical preacher endeavors to convert a frivolous girl to his ways of thinking, but is thwarted by his son who argues from a materialistic viewpoint.

(5)—A man endeavors to entrap his twin brother in order to shift the guilt for a crime through mistaken identity.

(6)—A man achieves wealth in order to win from his cousin the love of a girl, only to find that he has destroyed the girl's family in the process.

The student, in his study of the situations, is urged to concentrate on each subdivision and work out sketchy plot ideas, such as the above. In doing so, he may discover that he has created the nucleus of a plot which appeals to him—one that he deems worthy of development into a story.

Plotting, whether attacked through idea suggestion, as above, or whether through a process of bringing to the conscious mind ideas drawn from the reservoir of the subconscious, must be a task of sifting, viewing and reviewing. Unless an idea carries a spark of vitality, a lure, it should be discarded.

The appeal in using the "plot suggestion" system, as evolved through analyses of the situations, lies in the fact that at times the writer will seek futilely for plot "germs." In such cases, the slightest suggestion may awaken the imagination, give it the initial pressure to start the "mental motor" into action.

Chapter XVIII

FIFTEENTH SITUATION

Murderous Adultery

(Elements: *Two Adulterers; a Betrayed Husband or Wife*)

Famous usage of this Situation: *Paolo and Francesca* (Italian folklore and Episode from Dante's *Inferno*)

HERE we have a situation of practically no value for the screen, seldom attractive in the popular type of short stories, and withal, tragic and morbid. Censorship, of course, rules it out for the screen, unless very subtly handled. It can be used in pictures in the murder-mystery type of story, where the interest is centered on solving the problem of "who killed whom?" rather than on sordid details of an adulterous life led by the man or woman murdered.

In light novels this situation has found extensive use of late, and has been handled effectively in some books of deep and literary type.

The situation offers much more for the stage, and has been used many times through that medium, in ancient and modern drama.

When combined with Situation Thirty-three, *Erroneous Judgment,* there is even a possibility for usage of this situation in comedy, but never when applied in the seriousness as set forth by Polti. Naturally, in comedy treatment the husband or wife discovers that the respective mate did not commit adultery, that it was all a mistake—and no murder ensues.

It is not necessary to consume any length of time in dwelling on this situation. Its applications are very obvious. However, we will list a few factors. Murder need not serve as a culmination, except in using the subdivisions.

AN ADULTERER (*Motivating force*)	PARTY TO ADULTERY	BETRAYED WIFE OR HUSBAND	REASON
A childless queen	A peasant	The king	A child
A trapper's wife	Government official	A trapper	Loneliness
A nymphomaniac	Several men	The husband	Passion
(In risque stories)			
A girl afflicted with social disease	A detective	Detective's wife	Revenge
A politician	Wife of another politician	Husband of woman	Coercion

AN ADUL-TERER (Motivating force)	PARTY TO ADUL-TERY	BETRAYED WIFE OR HUSBAND	REASON
An amateur actress	Professional actor	Husband of actress	A career
A "casting director"	A job seeker (girl)	Husband of girl	Gross sensuality
Wealthy man	Poor girl	Girl's husband	Love
Poor girl	Wealthy man (Reversing motivating force)	Man's wife	Money
A crook	Wife of confederate	Confederate	Self-protection
An official	Wife of soldier	Soldier	Passion
A woman	A virile man	Invalid husband	A child

In most of the above, which in every case are "plots," when read from left to right, there is an element of sordidness. And yet we cannot get away from the fact that the situation offers one of life's greatest problems and is therefore extremely dramatic. And in all phases of art—painting, music or writing—it is just as essential to portray the sordid, earthly facts of life, as it is the lighter and more wholesome aspects. The writer cannot get away from truthful concepts, whether the picture presented is drab, ugly, or cheerful and uplifting. It is his duty to present life in all its different phases. This situation must be given the attention it deserves from that standpoint.

Subdivisions of the Fifteenth Situation:

A (1)—THE SLAYING OF A HUSBAND BY, OR
    FOR, A PARAMOUR
  (2)—THE SLAYING OF A TRUSTING LOVER
B   —THE SLAYING OF A WIFE FOR A PARA-
    MOUR AND IN SELF-INTEREST

The above subdivisions offer little except tragedy. They stress primitive passions and require great skill in treatment and finesse in writing. It might be well for the beginner to eschew these subdivisions entirely in his early work.

Chapter XIX

SIXTEENTH SITUATION

Madness

(Elements: *Madman* and *Victim*)

Famous usage of this Situation: *The Father* (Strindberg)

THERE is a fascination about the subject of "madness" which has led many writers to deal with it. But, in almost any form, it has little value on the screen, for like *Murderous Adultery,* it is unsuitable for picture production. Frequently it has been used in comedic way, but experience has proven that comedy based upon such a theme is ineffective. Representations of madness are too gruesome and too revolting to possess genuine entertainment value.

The above might very well apply, also, in fiction and on the stage. There is in all of us who cherish our sanity (in spite of realizing that we, too, may be a "little mad") a dread of facing the subject of madness. We know it exists, that our insane asylums are overflowing, and yet, as we would evade a contagious disease, we want to keep such realization in the background of our minds. Paradoxically, about the only way we keep our sanity is to reject from our minds thoughts of death, madness, incurable diseases, etc. A realization of the inevitability of disaster might very well lead to madness. Nature has given most of us this facility in discarding such morbid thoughts, for which we may be thankful. Therefore, instinctively we revolt against the subject of madness. It would be well for the student to study this situation from an academic standpoint rather than to strain to find in it a theme of popular appeal, except by using it with the idea of having a character brought to only temporary madness, through stress.

We will give a few factors, using as a third element in the triad, "The Cause."

MADMAN	VICTIM	THE CAUSE
Jealous woman	Her lover	Another woman
A miser	His nephew	Money
A wicked queen	A princess (Fairy tale formula)	Her lover
An explorer	His associate	Jungle heat
An aviator	His co-pilot	A woman
A peasant	A landlord	Poverty
A beast	A man	Self-protection
A treasure hunter	Another treasure hunter	The treasure
An ex-convict	His betrayer	Vengeance

MADMAN	VICTIM	THE CAUSE
Inmate of insane asylum	Superintendent of Asylum (Instinctive formula)	Insanity
A husband	Wife's lover (Familiar usage)	Adultery
A dictator	A small nation	Power
A preacher	His congregation	Fanaticism
A hermit	Another hermit	Isolation
A sea-captain	His crew	Insanity
A plantation-owner	His foreman	A native girl

As usual, the list could be extended endlessly. It will be noted that in most of the combinations suggested, only temporary madness has been stressed. Madness motivated by terror, jealousy, hatred, injustice, misguided leadership, and the like, offers much in the way of dramatic possibilities. Insanity as the result of a diseased brain, offers little.

Subdivisions of the Sixteenth Situation:

A (1)—KINSMEN SLAIN IN MADNESS
 (2)—A LOVER SLAIN IN MADNESS
 (3)—SLAYING OR INJURING OF A PERSON NOT HATED
B —DISGRACE BROUGHT UPON ONESELF THROUGH MADNESS
C —LOSS OF LOVED ONES BROUGHT ABOUT BY MADNESS

D   —MADNESS BROUGHT ON BY FEAR OF HEREDITARY INSANITY

The above subdivisions offer the more morbid phases of the situation. Their use by the beginning writer is not recommended.

Chapter XX

SEVENTEENTH SITUATION

Fatal Imprudence

(Elements: *The Imprudent; the Victim or the Object Lost*)

Famous usage of this Situation: *Blue Beard* (Perrault)

THIS situation is apt to be too morbid and unpleasant for the screen, in its purely dramatic phases, unless it is given subtle treatment, and modified by being combined with less harrowing situations. In its comedic phases, it has often been used with good effect.

In using the term "Fatal Imprudence," Polti did not mean necessarily that tragedy should ensue from its use. The situation, therefore, should not be viewed from this angle. Its application lies more in the field of comedy than tragedy.

Probably the most familiar and hackneyed usage of this situation is in the plot where the wife discovers her husband running around with a girl and displaying affection for her. She does something imprudent, such as starting divorce proceedings, taking on a young man in competition with her husband, or the like,—only to find that the girl is her husband's sister, who has returned from abroad.

This situation, on the whole, does not offer an overly satisfactory basis for truly entertaining, dramatic story plots. One of its principal usages has been in the realm of fantasy and fairy stories for children, where imprudence or curiosity leads the hero or heroine into conflict with witches, dwarfs, jungle creatures, and the like.

A still more important reason why this situation is not strong dramatically, is that "imprudence" and "curiosity" imply a certain weakness of character. And if not weakness, it infers that the story situation is based on someone's committing an act of folly which denotes a lack of dynamic force in the character. We find more interest in a character who proceeds in the full knowledge of what he is doing, than in one who does something accidentally, thoughtlessly or through sheer curiosity.

THE IMPRUDENT OR CURIOUS (Motivating force)	THE VICTIM (Or One Who Suffers)	OBJECT LOST
A bookkeeper	His wife	Bookkeeper's job
A stockbroker	His client	A fortune
A girl	Her sister	Sister's sweetheart

THE IMPRU-DENT OR CURIOUS (*Motivating force*)	THE VICTIM (*Or One Who Suffers*)	OBJECT LOST
An over-zealous detective	Another detective	Victim's life
A lawyer	His client	A law-suit
A gambler	His daughter	Money
Embezzling bank clerk	His sweetheart	Marriage
A farmer	His wife	The farm
Postoffice clerk	A girl	Love

(Implication being that clerk opens letter addressed to his sweetheart and takes some imprudent action which harms her)

A spy	His confederate	Confederate's life
Receiver of stolen goods	A crook	Liberty
A surgeon	One upon whom operation is performed	Surgeon's career
An adulterous wife	Her lover	A man's faith
A sheriff	His dog	A fugitive
An inventor	Innocent people	An invention
A mining engineer	Investors	A mine
A contractor	His employees	A dam
A politician	The public	Politician's career

From a study of the above factors, it will be seen that it is almost necessary to combine this situation with others in order to obtain a true plot. Take, for instance, the above elements "A surgeon" (Imprudent One), "One upon whom operation is performed" (Victim), and the Object Lost, the surgeon's career. We immediately assume that the surgeon through an imprudent experiment causes the death of the person upon whom he is operating, thereby destroying his career. A story based on such a slight structure would hardly hold the interest. It is necessary, therefore, to create other elements, to supply interest and suspense. If, for instance, the surgeon experimented with a new technique on his patient, at the instigation of a famous surgeon, his superior, and the technique failed, resulting in the patient's death, then we have created a dramatic situation. The surgeon is faced with the destruction of his own career if he keeps silent, or of destroying one he loves dearly if he tells the truth.

The student should not blindly assume that the above factors carry all the ingredients required for an entertaining plot. In this case, as in a number of others, the theme is indicated, but additional causes and factors must be drawn in to furnish complication and suspense.

Subdivisions of the Seventeenth Situation:

A (1)—IMPRUDENCE THE CAUSE OF ONE'S OWN MISFORTUNE
 (2)—IMPRUDENCE THE CAUSE OF ONE'S OWN DISHONOR

B (1)—CURIOSITY THE CAUSE OF ONE'S OWN MISFORTUNE

   (2)—LOSS OF THE POSSESSION OF A LOVED ONE, THROUGH CURIOSITY

C (1)—CURIOSITY THE CAUSE OF DEATH OR MISFORTUNE TO OTHERS

   (2)—IMPRUDENCE THE CAUSE OF A RELATIVE'S DEATH

   (3)—IMPRUDENCE THE CAUSE OF A LOVER'S DEATH

   (4)—CREDULITY THE CAUSE OF KINSMEN'S DEATHS

Subdivisions A (1), B (1), and (2), may be developed skillfully in comedy drama, and they are by no means hackneyed. Subdivisions C (1) (2) (3) and (4) offer little except morbid, tragic conceptions.

CHAPTER XXI

EIGHTEENTH SITUATION

Involuntary Crimes of Love

(Elements: *The Lover; the Beloved; the Revealer*)

Famous usage of this Situation: *Œdipus Rex* (Sophocles)

THIS situation, being solely dependent upon chance, has but little dramatic value. It is one of the most fantastic and implausible of the thirty-six. However, it seems to possess a great fascination for the average beginning writer, for the idea is submitted, in one phase or another, time after time, to the editors.

In this instance we will list the subdivisions before discussing the situation further, inasmuch as the elements may appear vague and indefinable at first reading. The subdivisions will elucidate the exact meaning intended by Polti.

A (1)—DISCOVERY THAT ONE HAS MARRIED ONE'S MOTHER

(2)—DISCOVERY THAT ONE HAS HAD A SISTER AS MISTRESS

B (1)—DISCOVERY THAT ONE HAS MARRIED
    ONE'S SISTER

  (2)—THE SAME CASE, IN WHICH THE
    CRIME HAS BEEN VILLAINOUSLY
    PLANNED BY A THIRD PARTY

  (3)—BEING UPON THE POINT OF TAKING
    A SISTER, UNKNOWINGLY, AS MIS-
    TRESS

C   —BEING UPON THE POINT OF VIO-
    LATING, UNKNOWINGLY, A DAUGH-
    TER

D (1)—BEING UPON THE POINT OF COMMIT-
    TING AN ADULTERY UNKNOWINGLY

  (2)—ADULTERY COMMITTED UNKNOW-
    INGLY

From a study of the above subdivisions, it will readily be seen that the situation involves censorable subjects. It might be possible to use some subtle suggestion of one of the subdivisions on the screen, but no
deliberate usage would be allowed.

In the field of fiction, this is one situation that has
had its day. It was used extensively in the classics and
during the time of Congreve when literature had de-
clined into a state of light frivolity.

Without being humorous, we are inclined to believe
that the principal use of this situation has been by amateur writers. For some unaccountable reason, the be-

ginner "discovers" this situation and becomes enthusiastic about the stabbing surprise when the hero discovers that he has unwittingly married his sister, fallen in love with his mother, whom he has not seen since childhood, or is on the point of seducing a girl relative when he discovers his error, sometimes through a locket around her neck, sometimes through a recognized heirloom, birthmark, etc.

Aside from the element of implausibility which surrounds the entire situation, it is basically disagreeable, almost nauseating. This being the case, we hardly believe that it is worthwhile to list any factors for it. We will let it lie in its slimy, black swamp, quiescent in the shadow of dripping boughs and tangled feelers.

CHAPTER XXII

NINETEENTH SITUATION

Slaying of a Kinsman Unrecognized

(Elements: The *Slayer;* the *Unrecognized Victim*)

Famous usage of this Situation: *Marie Tudor* (Hugo)

LIKE the preceding situation, this one is fundamentally implausible for it depends upon chance—the accidental failure of a character to recognize a kinsman.

Of it, Polti says: "Be it noted that Shakespeare has not in a single instance employed this Nineteenth Situation, an altogether accidental one, having no bearing upon his powerful studies of the will."

Again, for a proper understanding of the underlying meaning of this situation, we will list the subdivisions, before further discussion:

A (1)—BEING UPON THE POINT OF SLAYING A DAUGHTER UNKNOWINGLY, BY COMMAND OF A DIVINITY OR AN ORACLE

(2)—THROUGH POLITICAL NECESSITY

(3)—THROUGH A RIVALRY IN LOVE

(4)—THROUGH HATRED OF THE LOVER OF THE UNRECOGNIZED DAUGHTER

B (1)—BEING UPON THE POINT OF KILLING A SON UNKNOWINGLY

(2)—THE SAME CASE AS B (1), STRENGTHENED BY MACHIAVELLIAN INSTIGATIONS

(3)—THE SAME CASE AS B (2), INTERMIXED WITH HATRED OF KINSMEN

C   —BEING UPON THE POINT OF SLAYING A BROTHER UNKNOWINGLY

(1)—BROTHERS SLAYING IN ANGER

(2)—A SISTER SLAYING THROUGH PROFESSIONAL DUTY

D   —SLAYING OF A MOTHER UNRECOGNIZED

E   —A FATHER SLAIN UNKNOWINGLY, THROUGH MACHIAVELLIAN ADVICE

F (1)—A GRANDFATHER SLAIN UNKNOWINGLY, IN VENGEANCE AND THROUGH INSTIGATION

(2)—SLAIN INVOLUNTARILY

(3)—A FATHER-IN-LAW KILLED INVOLUNTARILY

G (1)—INVOLUNTARY KILLING OF A LOVED WOMAN

(2)—BEING UPON THE POINT OF KILLING
  A LOVER UNRECOGNIZED

(3)—FAILURE TO RESCUE AN UNRECOG-
  NIZED SON

This situation is not quite as sordid as Situation Eighteen, inasmuch as the crime or premeditated crime is not deliberate. Yet, the fact that whatever foul deed is perpetrated comes about through ignorance or unknowing, weakens the dramatic effect immeasurably. On the other hand, if the slayer recognized his victim and proceeded in his purpose, there could not possibly be any sympathy invoked for him. As it is, the slayer or one who attempts the slaying, may act righteously according to his own lights and is to be pitied when he learns the truth concerning the vicious act he has committed, or was about to commit.

When we pity a character for something he does, he loses his dynamic qualities. We can more readily pity the character against whom the crime is committed. In this situation it is necessary to pity *both* the slayer and the victim. This is bound to make the entire characterization weak and subjective.

Regardless of the above, the situation has been used to advantage in fiction and to some extent on the stage and screen. Generally, its use is very limited and should be brought into a plot only where, perchance, it falls naturally and inevitably.

It is not a situation with which to struggle valiantly to achieve the plot of a story which will be consistently appealing and logical. The element of chance or coincidence involved, as stated, is bound to weaken the plot structure. It might almost be compared to the use of an "act of God" to bring about a solution.

And right here it is timely to advise the student to avoid the use of lightning, earthquakes, floods and other elements of Nature to bring about the downfall of the antagonistic faction. True, "acts of God" have been used effectively in pictures and on the stage, as well as in stories—such as *The Hurricane, Father Malachy's Miracle, Run Little Chillun,* etc. The rule is not by any means a rigid one. But such procedure must be given the most subtle treatment, if used, and must be developed with every appearance of realism. If a storm is to become a vital factor in the conflict between the opposing forces, establish early in the story that the storm is brewing, that it is the time of the year for such a storm, hurricane, tornado, earthquake, or whatever the catastrophe may be. Also, if possible, use "acts of God" for the temporary downfall of the *protagonistic* forces rather than as a destructive one for the antagonistic faction.

Inasmuch as this Situation is not completely to be disregarded in plotting, we list a few factors, bringing in as the third element of the triad, *The Cause,* or the reason for the slaying or attempted slaying.

THE SLAYER (Or Person Premeditating a Slaying)	THE UNRECOGNIZED VICTIM	THE CAUSE
An Arctic explorer	His son (by a former wife) and a member of the party of exploration	Self-preservation
A detective	His brother, a crook	The law (or self-protection)
A night club singer	A cousin (Her friend's unprincipled lover)	The friend (lover)
A ruler	A spy (former sweetheart)	Military law
A native chief	His daughter	Sacrifice to a God
A sailor	His uncle, a sea-captain	Mutiny
An Indian chief	His adopted brother (white)	War
Captain of Firing Squad	His brother (a spy)	Duty

(In this case the recognition would come after the brother has faced the rifles of the firing squad)

A young man	His father, a "bon vivant"	Jealousy over a woman
A crooked contractor	His brother, a worker in an underground tunnel	Ruination of a competitor

The last triad will serve as adequately for an example as any of the others. The crooked contractor is bidding on a big construction job against a hated competitor. The only way he can win is to ruin the competitor. He hires some crooks to dynamite a tunnel under construction by the competitor. Unknowingly, the contractor's own brother (or son), has taken a job as laborer underground in the tunnel. Just prior to the explosion of the dynamite the contractor learns that his brother (or son) is below and will be killed when the explosion takes place, etc.

All very melodramatic, due to the fact that any plot worked out using this situation must necessarily be melodramatic, or tragic, or utterly implausible. In the above example, of course, the plot could be worked out happily by having the contractor go down into the tunnel, stop the dynamite from exploding and rescue his brother. It is not impossible to take even the most tragic or morbid situation and in some manner reconstruct it into a story which ends happily. This situation, for that reason, has its usefulness and should not be disregarded entirely.

Chapter XXIII

TWENTIETH SITUATION

Self-Sacrifice for an Ideal

(Elements: *The Hero; the Ideal; the "Creditor" or the Person or Thing Sacrificed*)

Famous usage of this Situation: *Romola* (George Eliot)

How quickly we turn now to an uplifting situation! No other situation, in fact, is as noble as this one, for sacrifice is the most beautiful and inspiring of human acts. What the ideal may be, whether political or religious, whether it be called Honor, or Piety, is of little importance. It exacts the sacrifice of all ties, of interest, passion, life itself! Because it is the basis of idealism, this situation may be used to excellent advantage on the screen, stage and in fiction, and is capable of many variations, yet it is by no means too hackneyed.

The elements listed above are a little obscure and so again we will give the subdivisions first before going into further discussion:

A (1)—SACRIFICE OF LIFE FOR THE SAKE OF ONE'S WORD

(2)—LIFE SACRIFICED FOR THE SUCCESS OF ONE'S PEOPLE

(3)—LIFE SACRIFICED IN FILIAL PIETY

(4)—LIFE SACRIFICED FOR THE SAKE OF ONE'S FAITH

B (1)—BOTH LOVE AND LIFE SACRIFICED FOR ONE'S FAITH

(2)—BOTH LOVE AND LIFE SACRIFICED TO A CAUSE

(3)—LOVE SACRIFICED TO INTERESTS OF STATE

C   —SACRIFICE OF WELL-BEING TO DUTY

D   —THE IDEAL OF "HONOR" SACRIFICED TO THE IDEAL OF "FAITH"

Note that each one of the subdivisions involves sacrifice in its highest form.

We can safely rave over the beauty of this situation, as it calls for the best in human nature. Maybe the transcendent feeling that goes with it is derived from a primitive source,—to the time many hundreds of years ago when sacrifices were offered to various Gods to placate them; sometimes a beauteous ceremony, sometimes an ugly one, where human life was sacrificed on an altar or the victim was flung into the jaws of a wild beast; but joyful or tragic, always beautiful and inspiring in the eyes of the devout.

Under this situation we find the ideal back of the

Crusades, the wars fought against the Infidels to regain possession of the Holy City—*Sacrifice for the Sake of One's Faith.*

Those Japanese soldiers who tied bombs around their waists and rushed over to the enemy lines, sacrificed their lives for an ideal.

Every day we hear of the heroic deeds of our Coast Guard, of our police,—all living exponents of "idealism."

The student cannot go wrong in giving much time and study to this situation and a proper application of it is bound to lead to a story worthy of the telling.

Below are some suggested factors for practice purposes:

THE HERO	THE IDEAL	THE "CREDITOR" OR PERSON OR THING SACRIFICED
An author	A theory of philosophy	Public opinion
An actress	Her daughter	Her stage career
A father	His son	Wealth
A newspaper editor	Public welfare	His brother
A general	Victory against enemies	His life
A missionary	His faith	Comforts of civilization
A politician	Honest government	Wealth

THE HERO	THE IDEAL	THE "CREDITOR" OR PERSON OR THING SACRIFICED
A composer	A versatile student	Composer's own career
An artist	His wife	Ambition
An automobile manufacturer	A racing car	His grandson
A wife	Her husband	Her husband's love
A girl	Her sister	Girl's lover
A fireman	His comrade	His life

The student will perceive that he can extend this list of his own volition without difficulty.

The factors of this situation can be blended admirably with the factors of almost any of the other situations, and yet in itself the situation carries all the necessary elements for an unending variety of worthwhile plots.

Chapter XXIV

TWENTY-FIRST SITUATION

Self-Sacrifice for Kindred

(Elements: *The Hero; the Kinsman; the "Creditor" or the Person or Thing Sacrificed*)

Famous usage of this Situation: *Damon and Pythias* (Camille)

THERE is a warm human quality in this situation that the preceding one lacks, but self-sacrifice for a relative or for a loved one has been used so much both in fiction and in photoplays that the idea has become exceedingly trite. To be effective, such material must be developed with distinction and novelty, and should be treated from a fresh viewpoint. To do this, the writer has to build up vital, human, real characterizations and make the relationship between them thoroughly convincing and interesting.

Although the sacrifice is more intimate in this situation, it lacks the breadth and scope of Situation Twenty. It is narrowed for the reason that it is more to be expected that one will sacrifice one's self for a mother, father, sister or brother; whereas self-sacrifice for humanity, or for a cause, is rarer and in its essence, more dynamic.

And yet in this natural human trait we find realism. We are able to get to the "heart of humanity" as it were. Take that popular series on the screen, *The Hardy Family,*—in it there is a constant phase of sacrifice for kindred, not of the tragic type, but nevertheless creating heart interest and a feeling of warmth towards all concerned.

In almost every novel, somewhere or another, will be found a nuance of this situation,—a mother sacrificing for a daughter; a brother for another brother; a father for a child; a sister for another sister, and so on. We are dealing then with a very important human trait and must give the situation the significance it deserves.

Many of the triads listed below are familiar, but undoubtedly capable of many new variations.

THE HERO	THE KINSMAN (For whom sacrifice is made)	THE "CREDITOR" OR THE PERSON OR THING SACRIFICED
A hobo	His brother	Freedom
A mother	Her daughter	A man's love
A man	His wife	His mistress
A mistress	Her lover	Her lover's wife
A youth	His mother	The father
A grandfather	His grandson	His life

THE HERO	THE KINSMAN (For *whom* sacrifice is made)	THE "CREDITOR" OR THE PERSON OR THING SACRIFICED
An Olympic contestant	His brother	Championship
A wealthy mother	Her improvident daughter	Wealth
A life-guard	His sweetheart	His life
A Jew (German resident)	His daughter	Wealth and liberty
A French Legionnaire	His brother	Liberty
A jewel thief	His child	Proceeds from crime
An invalid (suicide)	Her mother	Insurance money
A politician	His son, a murderer	Honor
A lawyer	His daughter (Accused of crime)	His mistress
A girl	Her father	Her virtue

Although probably not necessary, we will state again that in using the factors of this situation, it is required that an antagonistic faction be brought into the story to personify, or give reason for, the sacrifice. Take the last triad listed above: We know that the girl sacrifices her virtue, gives her body to someone to save her father from injury or disgrace. But that some one who forces her to this sacrifice is an integral part of the plot, the antagonist.

Subdivisions of the Twenty-First Situation:

A (1)—LIFE SACRIFICED FOR THAT OF A RELATIVE OR A LOVED ONE

   (2)—LIFE SACRIFICED FOR THE HAPPINESS OF A RELATIVE OR A LOVED ONE

B (1)—AMBITION SACRIFICED FOR THE HAPPINESS OF A PARENT

   (2)—AMBITION SACRIFICED FOR THE LIFE OF A PARENT

C (1)—LOVE SACRIFICED FOR THE SAKE OF A PARENT'S LIFE

   (2)—FOR THE HAPPINESS OF ONE'S CHILD, OR OF A LOVED ONE

   (3)—THE SAME SACRIFICE AS 2, BUT CAUSED BY UNJUST LAWS

D (1)—LIFE AND HONOR SACRIFICED FOR THE LIFE OF A PARENT OR A LOVED ONE

   (2)—MODESTY SACRIFICED FOR THE LIFE OF A RELATIVE OR A LOVED ONE

Chapter XXV

TWENTY-SECOND SITUATION

All Sacrificed for a Passion

(Elements: *The Lover; the Object of the Fatal Passion; the Person or Thing Sacrificed*)

Famous usage of this Situation: *Antony and Cleopatra* (Shakespeare)

In screen stories, this situation has been used chiefly in dealing with the downfall of a man or woman through dishonesty, infidelity or illicit projects. The demand for this type of material by film producers is not great. However, the situation can be effectively used merely as the premise of a plot, and the action developed along an entirely different line, after the idea of sacrifice for passion has been planted. Except in some such subordinate capacity, the situation is of little dramatic value in the screen play.

It may, however, be used in a comedic vein, when the "passion" is a mild and harmless one, such as a husband's "passion for poker," or a wife's "passion for clothes."

In fiction, there has been rather a wide usage of this situation, principally in the risqué type of novel, where the man or woman sacrifice all for pleasures of the flesh.

It has also been used very effectively on the stage, a striking example being that very successful stage play, *Rain,* wherein the missionary sacrifices his religious views and ultimately his life, in his craving for the body of a woman of ill repute.

This situation carries a powerful application in the affairs of humans. Pick up a newspaper and you will almost invariably find items pertaining to a murder committed on account of a woman; a raid on a gambling den; automobile fatalities through drunken driving; and the like. All such tragic happenings are brought about through sacrifice to a passion, whether that passion be drink, sex, easy money or other motives.

It is apparent then that this situation has a very human quality and is of great dramatic importance. It is basically tragic, as it portrays vividly the weaknesses of human character and is almost a direct antithesis of Situation Twenty, *Sacrifice for an Ideal.* In the latter the sacrifice is noble—while in this situation Twenty-two it is ignominious.

And yet how important is a situation of this kind in literature! If humanity lived on a plane of peace, honesty and understanding, minus vice and corruption, how limited would be the resources for the writer! He would have to go out of the realm of realism in order to create conflict, suffering and human depravity. So, perverting the old saying: "It's all grist for the typewriter."

Now for our suggested factors:

THE LOVER	OBJECT OF THE FATAL PASSION (Motivating force)	PERSON OR THING SACRIFICED
A public official	A frivolous woman	Honor
A soldier	A prostitute	Soldier's wife
A wealthy man	Gambling	Money
An aviator	Hazardous flying	His wife
A woman	Narcotics	A career
An actress	Fame	Her husband
An inventor	An invention	Mentality
An adventurer	Insurmountable mountain peak	His life
An actor	Race horses	A career
A man	Liquor	His child
(Formula of old play, "Ten Nights in a Barroom")		
A crook	A woman	His liberty
A business woman	A frivolous girl (Lesbian formula)	Woman's husband
A man	Another man (Homosexual formula)	A sweetheart
A miser	Gold	His child
A ruler	War	His country
A plantation owner	A native girl	His wife or sweetheart
A preacher	Religious dogma	His pastorate
A general	A woman spy	His regiment

In this situation, we have in many cases a perfect triad, with the typical hero or protagonist, as the person ruled by a passion; the object of the passion forming the motivating force, and the person sacrificed serving as the antagonist. It is interesting to note that the antagonist in this situation necessarily must struggle futilely, inasmuch as the person against whom he or she struggles, or the object of the fatal passion, must under the law of this situation, invariably win.

The question might well be asked: "Why not have the person chosen for sacrifice win out by bringing the protagonist back to realization of his error?" The answer to this question is very important. In every case we must abide by the laws governing the situation with which we are dealing. To do otherwise, is to destroy the value of the situation, to distort its true meaning. Each situation presents a clear-cut issue and were it otherwise the entire structure upon which the Thirty-six Situations are based would collapse.

And this means that even though the situations are combined to bring about greater novelty and more complications, *each factor must be true to the motivation given* under the situation in which such factor is listed. In other words, if you use the above factor, "Gold," as the Object of the Fatal Passion, and "A banker," a Malevolent Kinsman in Situation Thirteen, as the motivating force,—gold or wealth must be the fatal passion of the banker, and such gold or wealth must not be given any other interpretation.

Now, for instance, if you include as the third element of the triad, "a factory owner," Adversary in the Ninth Situation, such adversary must be a force actively engaged in combating the banker in his lust for gold. We have then a banker whose overwhelming passion is gold or wealth, being confronted with an adversary in the character of a factory owner, such adversary struggling to keep him from acquiring such wealth.

Subdivisions of the Twenty-second Situation:

A (1)—RELIGIOUS VOWS OF CHASTITY BROKEN FOR A PASSION
 (2)—A VOW OF PURITY BROKEN
 (3)—A FUTURE RUINED BY A PASSION
 (4)—POWER RUINED BY A PASSION
 (5)—RUIN OF MIND, HEALTH AND LIFE
 (6)—RUIN OF FORTUNES, LIVES, AND HONORS
B —TEMPTATIONS DESTROYING THE SENSE OF DUTY, OF PITY, ETC.
C (1)—DESTRUCTION OF HONOR, FORTUNE AND LIFE, BY EROTIC VICE
 (2)—THE SAME EFFECT PRODUCED BY ANY OTHER VICE

Subdivision A (1)—*Religious Vows of Chastity Broken for a Passion,* is exemplified in *The Garden of Allah,* Robert Hichens' famous work.

The life of Rasputin, the Russian Monk, typifies Subdivision A (4).

Faust sold his soul to the devil to appease his passion for a woman, and in that story of supreme sacrifice this situation reaches its greatest height.

It cannot be denied that in spite of certain inherent weaknesses in dramatic power, this situation is one of the most important of the thirty-six for the playwright or fictionist.

CHAPTER XXVI

TWENTY-THIRD SITUATION

Necessity of Sacrificing Loved Ones

(Elements: *The Hero; the Beloved Victim; the Necessity for the Sacrifice*).

Famous usage of this Situation: *Lucrèce Borgia* (Hugo)

THE chief use of this situation has been in classic drama. There are very few cases in modern life in which a character has felt the urgent necessity of sacrificing loved ones. The sense of duty is not so emotional and so intense today, as it was when the dramatists of Greece and Rome were writing their plays.

On the screen, in plays dealing with political matters, the situation has sometimes been used, as, for instance, when some official is compelled by a sense of duty to sacrifice a loved one. Frequently, in stories of this type, it may be employed, in a mild form, with good dramatic effect, but, in general, it is of little value for the screen, and not much more for the stage. In fiction it has its usefulness.

This situation, among several of the others, has become outmoded through the centuries. In the days when deities were looked upon with fear, awe and superstition, sacrifices became an obligation, a supreme function of life among the people. In the early Aztec civilization, the flower of youth was led to an altar, so that the priests could tear the heart from the body and place it in a crucible.

It can from this be understood how important this situation was at one time in literature, in the odes, paeans and in the drama.

With the rise of Christianity, sacrifice of loved ones became a sin against God and filial duty became the obligation of a true believer. "Honor Thy Father and Thy Mother . . ." one of the Ten Commandments.

Modern history has therefore placed a stigma on this situation and it is difficult to make it conform to our present pattern of living.

And yet, as in the case of each and every one of the situations, it has been used to great effect and will be used in the future, no doubt, in outstanding plays, pictures and works of fiction.

It is not our place to deny the applicability of any of the situations, but to view them in their true light, realize their limitations, and above all to be prepared to give subtle treatment to the ones which necessitate such handling.

THE HERO	THE BELOVED VICTIM	NECESSITY FOR SACRIFICE
A farmer	His daughter	Retention of property
(The old familiar melodramatic formula of "saving the old homestead.")		
A heartless mother	Her daughter	Wealth
A crook	Another crook (brother)	Self-preservation
A shipwrecked sailor	His comrade	Water
A mother	Her child	Another child
A sheriff	His brother, a crook	Duty
A wife	Her husband	Her father
A doctor	His cousin, blood donor	Doctor's injured daughter
A miner (Trapped in mine)	His brother (also trapped)	Miner's children
A man	His sweetheart	His mother
A mother	Her daughter	Daughter's step-father
An official	His son, a crook	Public welfare
Captain of a warship	His brother	Safety of vessel
A judge	His son, an embezzler	The law
A district attorney	His son (or brother)	An innocent suspect
Russian kulak	His father, accused of anti-Communism	Kulak's wife and family

THE HERO	THE BELOVED VICTIM	NECESSITY FOR SACRIFICE
A white woman	Her child—a half-breed	Family honor
A gangster	His sweetheart	Fidelity to his comrades

Among the above you will find listed several very familiar formulas, *i.e.,* the official who sacrifices his son, a crook, in order to fulfill his public duty; the district attorney who condemns his son, knowing he is guilty, in order to save an innocent victim, etc.

Such triads are given to impress upon the student just how this situation has been used to advantage many times in the past. And such factors *can* be used again if sufficient originality is given to the treatment. However, it would be our advice that the student choose less hackneyed elements, especially in his early work, as he is very apt, indeed, to fall into well-worn grooves should he do otherwise.

A (1)—NECESSITY FOR SACRIFICING A DAUGHTER IN THE PUBLIC INTEREST

   (2)—DUTY OF SACRIFICING HER IN FULFILLMENT OF A VOW TO GOD

   (3)—DUTY OF SACRIFICING BENEFACTORS OR LOVED ONES TO ONE'S FAITH

B (1)—DUTY OF SACRIFICING ONE'S CHILD,

UNKNOWN TO OTHERS, UNDER THE PRESSURE OF NECESSITY

(2)—DUTY OF SACRIFICING, UNDER THE SAME CIRCUMSTANCES, ONE'S FATHER

(3)—DUTY OF SACRIFICING, UNDER THE SAME CIRCUMSTANCES, ONE'S HUSBAND

(4)—DUTY OF SACRIFICING A SON-IN-LAW FOR THE PUBLIC GOOD

(5)—DUTY OF CONTENDING WITH A BROTHER-IN-LAW FOR THE PUBLIC GOOD

(6)—DUTY OF CONTENDING WITH A FRIEND

How splendidly some of the above nuances were used in the classics will be understood from the following exemplifications:

A (1), *Erechtheus,* by Euripides; B (1), *Melanippe,* by Euripides; B (2), *The Lemnian Women,* by Sophocles; B (5), *Horace,* by Corneille.

Chapter XXVII

TWENTY-FOURTH SITUATION

Rivalry of Superior and Inferior

(Elements: *The Superior Rival; the Inferior Rival; the Object*)

Famous usage of this Situation: *Strife* (Galsworthy)

This situation, typifying a clean-cut and vital struggle, is of almost equal effectiveness in comedy or drama. It makes a strong appeal to the sympathies of an audience because of its simple and direct dramatic quality. It lends itself to many combinations, chiefly Situation Number One, *Supplication;* Two, *Deliverance;* Three, *Crime Pursued by Vengeance;* Seven, *Falling Prey to Cruelty or Misfortune;* Thirty-three, *Erroneous Judgment,* and all of the situations dealing with *Sacrifice.* Consequently, it may be used as a splendid basic situation. It allows for vivid dramatic contrast, which is so necessary in the good screen story, stage play and work of fiction. It is especially effective for the radio, due to the clean, moral struggle involved.

The scope of this situation will be apparent in the factors which follow:

SUPERIOR RIVAL	INFERIOR RIVAL	THE OBJECT
Wealthy sportsman	Office clerk	A girl
A sea-captain	His first mate	A native girl
A ruler	A politician	Popular support
Owner of dress shop (woman)	A model	A man
District Attorney	Captain of police	The solving of a crime
A husband	Wife's former husband	Wife's love
A "star" salesman	Inexperienced salesman	Large order of goods
A ranch owner	A ranch foreman	A woman
(Popular Western formula)		
An aviator	A girl aviatrix	A contest
Wealthy woman	Her secretary	A man
A detective	A crook	Jewels
Chief of savage tribe	An adventurer	Leadership of tribe
A clever criminal	Gang of thieves	Loot
Famous actress	A business woman	Business woman's husband
Champion prize-fighter	A contender for title	The championship title
(Familiar sport story formula)		
A governor	Newspaper owner	Political issues
Plantation owner	A "share-cropper"	Owner's fiancee

SUPERIOR RIVAL	INFERIOR RIVAL	THE OBJECT
Wealthy oil man	Well driller	Oil man's daughter
Owner of pearl-fishing industry	Young native pearl diver	Native rule
A sheik	An archaeologist	Antiquities
A gang leader	A girl	Gang leader's brother

We will list below a few plot outlines which were created after momentary concentration on the factors:

(1)—A "star" salesman is endeavoring to land a large order of goods from a prominent buyer. His only competition is from an inexperienced young salesman sent out by a rival concern. While the star salesman is contacting the buyer, a peppery old man, the inexperienced salesman meets the daughter of the old man. He is urged by the daughter to play a part in an amateur play she has written, the player scheduled for the role having been taken ill and the young salesman being "the type." The daughter's career is at stake and when the young salesman learns that the old man is about to give the star salesman preference when purchasing the goods, he refuses to come to the rescue of the daughter, unless she forces her father to give him the business. The old man finally agrees. The young salesman plays the part exceedingly well. A Broadway producer witnesses the performance of the two young people and makes them an offer of a legitimate production if they will work together. The star salesman gets the order, the girl and youth gain a career, and fall in love, and the father has to accept the situation.

(2)—An aviator discovers that he is competing with a girl aviatrix in a cross country speed contest. He also finds that she is the former sweetheart of his best friend and had run out on this friend, causing the latter to throw up his career as a flyer and become a tramp.

The aviator is determined that the aviatrix shall not win the race, as he hates her for what she has done to his pal. He maintains a lead in the flight, with the girl a close second, after many obstacles have confronted both of them. While refueling, he learns that his friend is ill in the hospital and that the girl is trying to win the race in order to get money enough to pay for an operation which is necessary to save the friend's life.

Realizing that he had the girl all wrong, the aviator decides to throw the race to the girl. But after she has departed for the final stretch, he learns that his misguided mechanic, also a close friend of the invalid pal, had tampered with the girl's plane so that she will have to make a landing or bail out.

The aviator overtakes her and signals her to land. She believes he is trying to play a trick on her and refuses. He orders his mechanic and co-pilot to fly over her plane, and using a rope, he slides down into the cockpit of the girl's plane. The plane has just reached the end of the gasoline supply, and he and the girl are forced to land. In doing so the plane is wrecked. The co-pilot also lands in the aviator's plane and hurries to the rescue. The aviator is injured, and he tells the girl to take his plane and complete the flight. She refuses. He then informs her that *he* was the one who tampered with her plane and put it out of commission. When she learns this, she wrathfully climbs into his plane and leaves, winning the contest and the prize-money. Later she learns the truth, and of course, (pulp formula), she and the aviator realize that they are meant for each other, as does the best friend, who has come through his operation in tip top style, and gives them his blessing as well as his promise to take a proffered job.

The above outlines offer working bases for the popular types of story material, falling probably into the field of the "pulps," or in the first instance, for one of the "sales opportunity" magazines printing fiction.

We have continually endeavored to remain honest in citing examples of plots we create offhandedly from the triads, and in no case have we used the plots of any stories written by us, or previously published. We have tried to work with the factors in the same manner we expect the student to attack them.

Subdivisions of the Twenty-fourth Situation

A   —MASCULINE RIVALRIES
   (1)—OF A MAGICIAN AND AN ORDINARY
        MAN

(2)—OF A MORTAL AND AN IMMORTAL

(3)—OF CONQUEROR AND CONQUERED

(4)—OF SUZERAIN KING AND VASSAL KINGS

(5)—OF A KING AND A NOBLE

(6)—OF A POWERFUL PERSON AND AN UPSTART

(7)—OF RICH AND POOR

(8)—OF AN HONORED MAN AND A SUSPECTED ONE

(9)—RIVALRY OF TWO WHO ARE ALMOST EQUAL

(10)—RIVALRY OF EQUALS, ONE OF WHOM HAS IN THE PAST BEEN GUILTY OF ADULTERY

(11)—OF A MAN WHO IS LOVED AND ONE WHO HAS NOT THE RIGHT TO LOVE

(12)—OF THE TWO SUCCESSIVE HUSBANDS OF A DIVORCÉE

B (1)—OF A SORCERESS AND AN ORDINARY WOMAN

(2)—OF VICTOR AND PRISONER

(3)—OF QUEEN AND SUBJECT

(4)—OF A QUEEN AND A SLAVE

(5)—OF LADY AND SERVANT

(6)—OF A LADY AND A WOMAN OF HUMBLER POSITION

(7)—RIVALRY OF TWO WHO ARE ALMOST

EQUALS, COMPLICATED BY THE
ABANDONMENT OF ONE
(8)—RIVALRY BETWEEN A MEMORY OR
AN IDEAL (THAT OF A SUPERIOR
WOMAN) AND A VASSAL OF HER
OWN
(9)—RIVALRY OF MORTAL AND IMMOR-
TAL
C   —DOUBLE RIVALRY (A loves B, who loves
C, who loves D)

The student may find a wealth of ideas in the above
listed subdivisions. It is suggested, however, in attempting to use them for modern story plots, that triads
be formed and listed, as has been our practice. In following this procedure great care must be used to
modernize the classic interpretations.

CHAPTER XXVIII

TWENTY-FIFTH SITUATION

Adultery

(Elements: *A Deceived Husband or Wife; Two Adulterers*)

  Famous usage of this Situation: *The Scarlet Letter* (Hawthorne)

THIS situation has a genuine dramatic appeal if it is used skilfully and with the greatest discrimination. In itself it is too sensational and too salacious for screen purposes, but it may be effectively combined with Situations Thirty-two, *Mistaken Jealousy,* Thirty-three, *Erroneous Judgment,* or Thirty-four, *Remorse.* By such combinations it will possess the strength and interest of the basic conflict of *Adultery,* without disagreeable and unpleasant developments.

  If the student writer finds his theme and characterization strong enough to warrant the use of this situation, the inherent conflicts should be given subtle treatment and the greatest care should be taken to guard against setting forth the action in a crude and depressing fashion. The best effect may be obtained by suggestion and implication, as for instance in the well worked out theme of a motion picture, the name of which we do not recall, wherein the conflict of the situation was handled by incorporating the divorce, marriage, divorce and remarriage of the principals.

In our present-day popular novels and in books of high literary quality, adultery has been used effectively and powerfully.

The subject of adultery is, of course, strictly sexual. According to the conventions of our civilization, it represents a relationship between individuals not legally authorized to enter into such relationship. Whether that association is sinful or not depends largely upon the motivation. In the accepted use of the word "adultery," it implies an immoral sexual relationship and a betrayal of a lawful husband or wife. And yet, an adulterous situation might exist and win the entire approval and sympathy of the reader or an audience.

Adultery relies on the basic emotions of love and passion and therefore has a very definite place in fiction. To the sensitive writer it may be a subject which he will find difficulty in handling. But a writer should never allow his personal opinions or prejudices to enter into his "writing mentality." It is within his field as an author to write of life as it is, and not necessarily as he would have it.

The following factors should afford many ideas for

powerful fiction material, especially when combined, as stated, with other situations.

AN ADUL-TERER (Motivating Force)	COM-PANION IN ADULTERY	PERSON BETRAYED	THE CAUSE
A king	An actress	The queen	Passion
A banker	His secretary	His mistress	Revenge
An heiress	Her riding master	Her fiance	Lust
Riding master	An heiress	His wife	Money
Vaudeville actor	His partner	Partner's husband	Hatred for husband
A world traveler (male)	A tourist (girl)	Girl's fiance	Obsession for virginity
A salesman (a bigamist)	Unlawful wife	Lawful wife	Perversion
An artist's model	Another model	Second model's husband	Lesbianism
A crook	Respected woman	Woman's husband	Glamour
A hunchback	A girl	Girl's fiance	Eroticism
A preacher	A "party" girl	Preacher's wife	Prudery of wife
A woman	A male escort	Woman's husband	Latter's impotency
A prostitute	A politician	Politician's wife	Blackmail premeditated

(Note: "Lust" and "Money" are joined by a brace to indicate they relate together.)

AN ADUL-TERER (Motivating Force)	COM-PANION IN ADULTERY	PERSON BETRAYED	THE CAUSE
A native girl	An engineer	Engineer's fiancee	Superiority over natives
A business woman	A salesman	Long absent husband	Loneliness

(Variation of "Enoch Arden" situation)

It will be noted that most of the above triads, with their motivations and causes, offer vivid, human dramas —sordid, to be sure, in every case, and yet problems faced by people in various strata of life and based largely on that great determining factor—sex.

Subdivisions of the Twenty-fifth Situation

A   —A MISTRESS BETRAYED
  (1)—FOR A YOUNG WOMAN
  (2)—FOR A YOUNG WIFE
  (3)—FOR A GIRL
B   —A WIFE BETRAYED
  (1)—FOR A SLAVE, WHO DOES NOT LOVE IN RETURN
  (2)—FOR DEBAUCHERY
  (3)—FOR A MARRIED WOMAN (A DOUBLE ADULTERY)
  (4)—WITH THE INTENTION OF BIGAMY
  (5)—FOR A YOUNG GIRL, WHO DOES NOT LOVE IN RETURN

(6)—A WIFE ENVIED BY A YOUNG GIRL WHO IS IN LOVE WITH HER HUSBAND

(7)—BY A COURTESAN

(8)—RIVALRY BETWEEN A LAWFUL WIFE WHO IS ANTIPATHETIC AND A MISTRESS WHO IS CONGENIAL

(9)—BETWEEN A GENEROUS WIFE AND AN IMPASSIONED GIRL

C (1)—AN ANTAGONISTIC HUSBAND SACRIFICED FOR A CONGENIAL LOVER

(2)—A HUSBAND, BELIEVED TO BE LOST, FORGOTTEN FOR A RIVAL

(3)—A COMMONPLACE HUSBAND SACRIFICED FOR A SYMPATHETIC LOVER

(4)—A GOOD HUSBAND BETRAYED FOR AN INFERIOR RIVAL

(5)—FOR A GROTESQUE RIVAL

(6)—FOR AN ODIOUS RIVAL

(7)—FOR A COMMONPLACE RIVAL, BY A PERVERSE WIFE

(8)—FOR A RIVAL LESS HANDSOME, BUT USEFUL

D (1)—VENGEANCE OF A DECEIVED HUSBAND

(2)—JEALOUSY SACRIFICED FOR THE SAKE OF A CAUSE

E   —A HUSBAND PERSECUTED BY A REJECTED RIVAL

The above subdivisions will offer ideas for many additional triads. They offer almost every conceivable form of depravity, deserving of a master such as Havelock Ellis when treated from a psychological standpoint. But to the story writer, the principal lesson they teach is caution as to their use, especially for stories slanted for the screen.

CHAPTER XXIX

TWENTY-SIXTH SITUATION

Crimes of Love

(Elements: *The Lover; the Beloved*)

Famous usage of this Situation: *Moll Flanders* (Defoe)

OF EVEN less dramatic value than Situation Eighteen, *Involuntary Crimes of Love,* this situation deals with depressing, diseased and psychopathic manifestations. The only subdivisions that may be developed for screen story purposes, with good effect, are B (1), (2), C (1). Even these must be used in combination with other situations that relieve the depressing effect.

We make it a point to stress screen values of the situations, inasmuch as we want to impress upon the student that large financial returns accrue from sales of material to the screen, and it is a medium to keep in mind constantly, for possible additional profits from fiction writing.

In general, this Situation should be avoided when intentionally slanting a story for the screen. Some of the nuances as set forth in the subdivisions are hackneyed and unattractive and even if combined with other situations are apt to create a trite and depressing plot.

In order to present a clearer meaning of this situation, we list the subdivisions:

A (1)—A MOTHER IN LOVE WITH HER SON
　(2)—A DAUGHTER IN LOVE WITH HER FATHER
　(3)—VIOLATION OF A DAUGHTER BY A FATHER
B (1)—A WOMAN ENAMORED OF HER STEPSON
　(2)—A WOMAN AND HER STEPSON ENAMORED OF EACH OTHER
　(3)—A WOMAN BEING THE MISTRESS, AT THE SAME TIME, OF A FATHER AND A SON, BOTH OF WHOM ACCEPT THE SITUATION
C (1)—A MAN BECOMES THE LOVER OF HIS SISTER-IN-LAW
　(2)—A BROTHER AND A SISTER IN LOVE WITH EACH OTHER

A brief study of the above will indicate the generally sordid aspect of the situation. Subdivision A (1), for instance, is of little or no use in any form of story writing, inasmuch as the mother's love for her son cannot under the laws of this situation be other than a depraved, unnatural type of affection. This situation dwells on *crimes* of love, and not on the beautiful affection generally bestowed by a mother on her offspring.

One might almost automatically ask the question: "Why did Polti include such a revolting situation in his compilation?" The answer is obvious. In dwelling on fundamentals, the bad have to go with the good, just as certain plants are edible and nourishing and others are deadly poison.

Subdivision C (2)—a brother and sister in love with each other—represents another idea that is seized upon so many times by the new writer. It is practically always used by the beginner, however, where the relationship is not known until a sexual union is about to be consummated, or a marriage planned. The favorite device is to have the boy discover a picture of his mother in a locket dangling from the girl's neck—just soon enough to prevent incest from taking place. Or maybe she has a birthmark on her left shoulder that identifies her as his long lost sister! The denouement is naturally that the boy and girl realize that their affection was a brotherly and sisterly one and not the sort of love experienced by persons intending to marry; which makes it all very sweet and wholesome—and utterly trite and stupid, as well as being based on coincidence stretched to the "nth" degree.

The one word title for this Situation, if we dare to correct Polti, should be *Incest*. Strive as hard as you like, it is difficult to make the subject entertaining. It is too revolting to the healthy mind. The only nuance of the situation that allows of fairly normal treatment is C (1)—a man becomes the lover of his sister-in-law. This might happen in the best of families; in fact, it does. But even at that, the subject is not particularly edifying or entertaining. It would be just as simple for the man to fall in love with somebody else's sister-in-law and take her as his mistress. The relationship offers but slight dramatic advantage.

In Rabelaisian comedy, Subdivision B (3)—a woman being the mistress, at the same time, of a father and a son, both of whom accept the situation—might offer some amusing situations. At least it affords the only touch of lightness to the drab effect produced by this reflection of human behavior.

We can see no great purpose to be served in attempting to list factors for this situation, and suggest that its only use should be when it falls naturally into the plot, where a novel portraying the raw side of human nature is contemplated.

CHAPTER XXX

TWENTY-SEVENTH SITUATION

Discovery of the Dishonor of a Loved One

(Elements: *The Discoverer; the Guilty One*)

Famous usage of this Situation: *Esther Waters* (George Moore)

This situation offers opportunity for new and interesting developments, especially in subdivisions A (1), A (2), D (5) and D (6), as follows:

A (1)—DISCOVERY OF A MOTHER'S SHAME
   (2)—DISCOVERY OF A FATHER'S SHAME
   (3)—DISCOVERY OF A DAUGHTER'S DISHONOR
B (1)—DISCOVERY OF A DISHONOR IN THE FAMILY OF ONE'S FIANCEE
   (2)—DISCOVERY THAT ONE'S WIFE HAS BEEN VIOLATED BEFORE MARRIAGE: SINCE THE MARRIAGE
   (3)—THAT SHE HAS PREVIOUSLY COMMITTED A FAULT

(4)—DISCOVERY THAT ONE'S WIFE HAS FORMERLY BEEN A PROSTITUTE

(5)—DISCOVERY OF DISHONOR ON THE PART OF A LOVER

(6)—DISCOVERY THAT ONE'S MISTRESS, FORMERLY A PROSTITUTE, HAS RETURNED TO HER OLD LIFE

(7)—DISCOVERY THAT ONE'S LOVER IS A SCOUNDREL, OR THAT ONE'S MISTRESS IS A WOMAN OF BAD CHARACTER. THE SAME DISCOVERY CONCERNING A SO-CALLED KING

(8)—THE SAME DISCOVERY CONCERNING ONE'S WIFE

C   —DISCOVERY THAT ONE'S SON IS AN ASSASSIN

D (1)—DUTY OF PUNISHING A SON WHO IS A TRAITOR TO COUNTRY: A BROTHER WHO IS A TRAITOR TO HIS PARTY

(2)—DUTY OF PUNISHING A SON CONDEMNED UNDER A LAW WHICH THE FATHER HAS MADE

(3)—DUTY OF PUNISHING A SON BELIEVED TO BE GUILTY

(4)—DUTY OF SACRIFICING, TO FULFILL A VOW OF TYRANNICIDE, A FATHER UNTIL THEN UNKNOWN

(5)—DUTY OF PUNISHING A BROTHER WHO IS AN ASSASSIN
(6)—DUTY OF PUNISHING ONE'S MOTHER TO AVENGE ONE'S FATHER

From a study of the above subdivisions of this situation, it will be seen that in its more subtle forms, it possesses a dramatic value unequaled by any of the situations except the four dealing with self-sacrifice. But the student-writer should here, again, guard against giving such material as this, sensational, exaggerated, implausible development. The human element should be emphasized, and the characterizations drawn with fine, clear-cut strokes.

Subdivisions B (1), B (5) and B (7) are susceptible of comedic treatment.

The principal reason for the attractiveness of this situation is because it lies generally within the scope of family life, thus arousing poignant heart interest. What a telling blow to the relatives of a loved one to find that he or she has committed a dishonorable or shameful deed! How keen the anguish of the guilty one upon realization of the pain and suffering caused to those dear to him! Here, possibly, lies the greatest punishment for the criminal—more than chains and bars, because the latter shackle his body, the former, his soul.

Subdivision B (7)—*Discovery that One's Lover is a Scoundrel*—has been used very extensively in "true story" magazines; the unsophisticated girl meets the suave, glittery play-boy and falls for him, quite often granting him her "all." She overlooks the purity and integrity of her commonplace, hard-working lover, in the process of being wooed by the scoundrel, but later, you may be sure, she will realize her error and return to the bosom of the boy who understands.

Subdivision D (2)—*Duty of Punishing a Son Condemned Under a Law Which the Father Has Made* —has occurred many times in real life and confers glory upon the parent; in fiction and on the screen it has been used so much that it requires very unusual treatment to revive its inherent dramatic value.

In listing the factors of this situation, it is necessary to complete the dramatic triad, by including the missing element—motivation. In "Discoverer," we have the person who finds out about the shame of a loved one; in "Guilty One" we have the one committing the sin or crime. Now we must supply the motive for the sin or crime; otherwise, the situation will be left up in the air, nebulous and offering an unanswered riddle. We will entitle the motivating cause of the sin or crime, "The Reason," whether it be a person, object or purpose.

THE DISCOVERER	THE GUILTY ONE	THE REASON
A son	His mother, a woman of ill-fame	Money
A daughter	Her father, a murderer	Hatred for a rival

THE DISCOVERER	THE GUILTY ONE	THE REASON
A girl	Her lover, an embezzler	Another woman
A wife	Her husband	A hidden crime

(The interpretation of the triad should in all
cases follow a pattern, such as in this case:
A wife discovers her husband to be guilty of
a crime which he has kept a secret from her.)

A husband	His wife	A sinful past
A father	His son, a murderer	Jealousy over a woman
A senator	His son, a traitor	A woman spy
A farmer	His daughter, *enceinte*	A tramp
A detective	His son, a thief	Hatred for father's occupation
A doctor	His nurse, a modern Borgia	A psychic complex
A Gypsy leader	His sweetheart	Passion for a nobleman
A Kentucky moonshiner	His son, a traitor to the family	Daughter of feuding neighbor

(Familiar "Kentucky feud" formula)

A reporter	His father, a banker	Embezzlement to cover losses
A stock broker	His wife	Her secret aid to a rival, her lover
A judge	His son, a murderer	Heritage of murderous instincts from mother

THE DISCOVERER	THE GUILTY ONE	THE REASON
An architect	His brother, a crooked contractor	Money
Officer of the law	His son, a smuggler	Preservation of father's life

For practice purposes, we suggest that the student-writer work out rough outlines for plots, using the above triads. After this has been done, write them again supplying different motivations; for instance, in the last mentioned triad, instead of the son becoming a smuggler in order to protect his father's life which is threatened by the smuggling gang, he may have become a smuggler for the purpose of showing his father that he could convict the gang through direct action rather than more methodic procedures.

This practice work will tend to give increased facility in building plots from suggested characterizations and motivations.

Chapter XXXI

TWENTY-EIGHTH SITUATION

Obstacles to Love

(Elements: *Two Lovers; an Obstacle*)

Famous usage of this Situation: *The Garden of Allah* (Robert Hichens)

THE chief screen value of this situation lies in comedy-drama and straight comedy. It may also be used as the basis for melodrama, though, in its melodramatic phases, it is rather trite. It is safe to say that perhaps fifty percent of the comedy-dramas that have been produced have been combinations of Situation Twenty-eight and Thirty-three, *Erroneous Judgment*. While the more obvious obstacles have been exhausted by too frequent use, there are still many variations that can be devised to separate or estrange lovers, so that, in general, the situation is relatively fresh.

In the field of fiction, it is safe to say that more stories have been written based upon this situation than any of the others. That situation which is quoted continually as a stock example: "Boy meets girl; boy falls in love with girl; boy wins girl," falls well within the scope of this basic situation.

It would be difficult to imagine what the writer would do without being able to resort to this situation! A goodly majority of the stories in the higher bracket magazines are clever variations of it. And why not? It offers one of the principal motivations of all peoples, regardless of class or color. It started back with Adam and Eve, if we accept a literal interpretation of the Biblical story. That was the beginning of the "boy meets girl" angle and the inception of our present situation *Obstacles to Love*.

When a cave man wanted his woman, he took a club and went out and got her, if he happened to be stronger than the other fellow who had his eyes on her. The obstacle confronting our hero cave man, therefore, was in the person of another cave man, and the conflict was purely physical and not mental. We have advanced somewhat since that time and have given the protagonist and antagonist more or less intellectuality, except in the case of certain types of action stories. In these, the physical conflict stands in its age-old position.

From the above the student will appreciate the value of a study of the following triads, and his own additions to the list.

THE BELOVED

A LOVER (*Motivating force*)	*(Object of affections)*	OBSTACLE (*Antagonist*)
A poor musician	Grand opera singer	Social barriers
A cowhand	Ranchowner's daughter	Society man

(Familiar "Western" formula)

A truck driver	An author (woman)	Intellectual barriers
A secretary	Her employer	Employer's wife

(Familiar "True story" formula)

A creole	A white plantation owner	Racial prejudice

(Old "Southern story" formula)

A sea-captain	A girl	His occupation
A member of royalty	A servant	Social barriers
A servant (girl)	Member of royalty or socialite	Social barriers

(The above two triads represent the familiar
"Cinderella" formula, where the girl meets
her "prince charming," realizes the social
gap, but he weds her anyway; or vice versa)

A man	A girl	Betrothal of girl
A girl	A man	Betrothal of man
A chauffeur	A debutante	Her mother
A man, divorced	A young girl	Religion
A girl	A married man	His marriage
A cripple (man)	Healthy young girl	Physical barrier
An impotent man	A woman	Sexual incapacity

THE BELOVED

A LOVER (Motivating force)	(Object of affections)	OBSTACLE (Antagonist)
A high-strung girl	A stunt flyer	Fear
	(Formula of man's dangerous position preventing marriage)	
A hermit	A woman	Vow of celibacy
A man	A woman	Inherited disease
A woman lawyer	A politician	A career
A young girl	An old man	Age

It is unnecessary to carry the list further. The triads possible to work out under the above headings are endless. The difficulty lies in conceiving elements which have not been overdone. And yet there is not a single one of the above triads that could not be treated in a novel and entertaining manner. The student may very well be optimistic of a sale of such a story, as the groundwork is firm and tried, and when built upon intelligently and with a touch of originality, the story structure will be viewed by the majority of readers with approval.

Subdivisions of the Twenty-Eighth Situation

A (1)—MARRIAGE PREVENTED BY INEQUALITY OF RANK

   (2)—INEQUALITY OF FORTUNE AN IMPEDIMENT TO MARRIAGE

B   —MARRIAGE PREVENTED BY ENEMIES AND CONTINGENT OBSTACLES

C (1)—MARRIAGE FORBIDDEN ON ACCOUNT
OF THE YOUNG WOMAN'S PREVIOUS
BETROTHAL TO ANOTHER

(2)—THE SAME CASE, COMPLICATED BY
AN IMAGINARY MARRIAGE OF THE
BELOVED OBJECT

D (1)—A FREE UNION IMPEDED BY THE OP-
POSITION OF RELATIVES

(2)—FAMILY AFFECTION DISTURBED BY
THE PARENTS-IN-LAW

E   —BY THE INCOMPATIBILITY OF TEM-
PER OF THE LOVERS

Most of the above nuances have been covered in the
triads listed.

Chapter XXXII

TWENTY-NINTH SITUATION

An Enemy Loved

(Elements: *The Beloved Enemy; the Lover; the Hater*)
Famous usage of this Situation: *The Bride of Lammermoor* (Scott)

THIS situation has been used extensively in pictures, principally in innumerable Western melodramas, and in "feud" stories of various locales.

It is a situation which the student must approach warily. Unless he handles it from an original viewpoint, and develops it in a distinctive, novel fashion, it will very aptly fall into well-worn grooves.

In fiction, its common usage has been where the father of the girl has utter contempt for the hero, the girl's lover. It falls almost naturally into the sphere of comedy, as the father's hatred is very likely to develop a humorous quality, willy-nilly. It is difficult to take seriously the arbitrary attitude of the parent, especially if the lover happens to be a likeable young chap.

Using the reverse of the above, we have the famous "mother-in-law" situation. In this case, the mother of the *Beloved Enemy,* the wife, carries a grudge or hatred against her son-in-law, the *Lover*.

Broad interpretation must be given to the element, *Beloved Enemy*. The wife in the above case is certainly not an enemy, only in the aspect that she is the daughter of an enemy to the *Lover,* or husband.

In recent times we have a splendid example of a true-life application of this situation. We refer to the marriage of the former king of England, now the Duke of Windsor, to Mrs. Wally Simpson, an American woman. Possibly no element of real hatred was involved in this affair, but the Duke's mother and brother most certainly opposed the match, placing Mrs. Simpson in the position of Beloved Enemy, the Duke of Windsor as the Lover, and his mother and brother as the Haters.

This situation, as stated, is rather misleading when it comes to a literal interpretation of the elements. The intention in the majority of the nuances is decidedly not that the Lover loves an Enemy. The true meaning is that the Lover loves a person whose kindred are antagonistic towards him and his love motive.

For greater immediate understanding of the situation, we will list the subdivisions before going into further discussion.

A   —THE LOVED ONE HATED BY KINSMEN
        OF THE LOVER

 (1)—THE LOVER PURSUED BY THE BROTH-
        ERS OF HIS BELOVED

(2)—THE LOVER HATED BY THE FAMILY OF HIS BELOVED

(3)—THE LOVER IS THE SON OF A MAN HATED BY THE KINSMEN OF HIS BELOVED

(4)—THE BELOVED IS AN ENEMY OF THE PARTY OF THE WOMAN WHO LOVES HIM

B (1)—THE LOVER IS THE SLAYER OF THE FATHER OF HIS BELOVED

(2)—THE BELOVED IS THE SLAYER OF THE FATHER OF HER LOVER

(3)—THE BELOVED IS THE SLAYER OF THE BROTHER OF HER LOVER

(4)—THE BELOVED IS THE SLAYER OF THE HUSBAND OF THE WOMAN WHO LOVES HIM, BUT WHO HAS PREVIOUSLY SWORN TO AVENGE THAT HUSBAND

(5)—THE SAME CASE, EXCEPT THAT A LOVER, INSTEAD OF A HUSBAND, HAS BEEN SLAIN

(6)—THE BELOVED IS THE SLAYER OF A KINSMAN OF THE WOMAN WHO LOVES HIM

(7)—THE BELOVED IS THE DAUGHTER OF THE SLAYER OF HER LOVER'S FATHER

It will be seen that all the subdivisions listed under "B" involve a slaying. In such, the Beloved may very well become an Enemy when the murder of a kinsman of the Lover takes place.

We believe the student will work better using the titles, The Beloved, The Lover, and The Hater, omitting the word "Enemy" from the first listed factor.

THE BELOVED (Subjective force)	THE LOVER (Motivating force)	THE HATER (Antagonistic force)
An heiress	A poor law clerk	Father of heiress
Daughter of a Kentucky "moonshiner"	Rival "moonshiner"	Girl's family

(Familiar "Kentucky feud" formula)

Politician's daughter	Son of Politician's enemy	The Politician
A preacher's son	A dance hall girl	The preacher
A commoner (woman)	Member of royalty	Latter's family

(The above-mentioned "Windsor-Simpson" situation)

A murderer	A girl	Her brother, friend of the victim
A circus girl	A lion tamer	Lion tamer's brother
A city girl	A prospector	Prospector's partner

(Motive: Girl's efforts to lure prospector from his work)

A soldier	A girl (of enemy country)	Soldier's family

THE BELOVED (Subjective force)	THE LOVER (Motivating force)	THE HATER (Antagonistic force)
A murderer	A woman, whose husband is victim	Husband's brother
An apache (girl)	An apache	Girl's former sweetheart
A husband	His wife	Wife's mother
	(Familiar "mother-in-law" situation)	

We have not deemed it necessary to set forth a long list of triads, as it will undoubtedly be beneficial for the student to create new factors for himself. This practice, in itself, will gradually tend to increase the efficiency in becoming "plot minded."

Chapter XXXIII

THIRTIETH SITUATION

Ambition

(Elements: *An Ambitious Person; a Thing Coveted; an Adversary*)

Famous usage of this Situation: *Julius Caesar* (Shakespeare)

"Ambition, one of the most powerful of passions, if it be not indeed the passion par excellence will always affect the spectator strongly, for he feels and knows that, once awakened in a man, it will cease only with his death. And how many are the objects of its desire! Tyrannical power, high rank, honors, fortune (by inheritance, marriage, robbery, etc.), the conservation of riches (avarice), glory (political, scientific, literary, inventive, artistic), celebrity, distinction."

This situation could not be analyzed more aptly than in the above quotation from Polti. It is a remarkable thing that this situation, which is suggestive of plots dealing with the basic emotional conflicts of humanity, has been practically ignored by the modern dramatists. It offers the playwright, the writer of screen stories and the fictionist a wide range of material that may be developed dramatically and interestingly.

Next to the situations having the supreme emotional passion, love, as a basis, this situation might very well take second place in power and scope. After all, just what are the most impressive and lasting motives of human beings? From the physical or primitive standpoint, we struggle from the time of birth for food. This struggle carries on until death. In one way or another we fight to feed our bodies. And even in this elemental human demand, ambition creeps in—ambition to acquire the means to satisfy the physical hunger adequately and satisfactorily. "It's nice to eat," the saying goes. It is generally offered lightly and said with a smile, but it comes from the heart. And some form of ambition is necessary to even acquire or take care of one's physical wants, whether that ambition is to go "on relief" or acquire a million dollars.

The next basic motive for continuing to live and survive is *love*—whether that love be of a sexual nature, spiritual seeking, love of power, wealth, fame, etc., or a combination of several or all. And to achieve this love objective requires *ambition,* urge, struggle, whether in a minor or major degree.

Ambition then is an integral part of our nature for in one sense of the word, struggle of any sort is ambition —a desire to attain something.

Ambition involves a conflict. This may seem a broad

statement, but it is true. Nothing is attained without conflict in some degree. The conflict may be a struggle within one's self against lethargy, physical weakness, or inhibitions; it may be a struggle to prove oneself physically and mentally capable of doing a certain job or piece of work; it may be a fight against a wild beast, an enemy in battle; a struggle with a person seeking to profit from individual enterprise. In love between man and woman, which is based on *ambition,* there is conflict, struggle, and union is only attained through individual achievement.

We have dwelt on this motivating force, ambition, to some extent, in order that the student will realize its importance in dramatic construction. In dealing with fundamental principles as we are doing in studying the Thirty-six Situations, a realization must be had of their true meaning and value. And the result of such study will result in an awakening to the fact that the entire field of psychology has been embraced and touched upon!

And now for some suggested triads:

AN AMBITIOUS PERSON	*A THING COVETED*	*AN ADVERSARY*
An art collector	Masterpiece of art	Rival collector
A student	A degree	Poverty
A man	A woman's love	Another man

(Probably the simplest and yet most powerful triad in all literature)

AN AMBITIOUS PERSON	A THING COVETED	AN ADVERSARY
A criminal	Wealth	The law
A dictator	A country	Rival powers
An office clerk	A higher position	Another clerk
An explorer	Unknown territory	Natural barriers
A politician	An office	Another politician
A cattle rustler	Herd of cattle	A cowhand
A scientist	An anti-toxin	Another scientist
A prize-fighter	A championship	Rival contender
A miser	Gold	His daughter
An author	Literary master-piece	Ill-health
A lion	Food	A grizzly-bear
A lawyer	A judgeship	Presiding judge
A farmer	A crop	Natural elements
A crook	A jewel	A detective
A mother	Daughter's love	The father
A sultan	A white girl	Sultan's subjects
A spiritual leader	Peace	Militarists

Although the factors in this situation may be blended with certain factors in other situations, this will not be necessary, inasmuch as we have here the complete basis for innumerable plots, an inexhaustible supply. Conceive any type of character with a supreme ambition, place obstacles and adversaries in his path, and have him fight on through to attainment—and you have a story. The locale can be any place on earth, for in every land and among every class and color of people, there is ambition and antagonistic forces. Yes, even in the Arctic regions, an Eskimo may have ambitions to become the greatest fisherman of his tribe and among that tribe will be some one who will resent and combat his attempt!

Polti evidently did not consider it necessary to create many subdivisions for this situation, as he lists but a few, as follows:

A   —AMBITION WATCHED AND GUARDED AGAINST BY A KINSMAN OR A PATRIOT FRIEND

(1)—BY A BROTHER

(2)—BY A RELATIVE OR PERSON UNDER OBLIGATION

(3)—BY PARTISANS

B   —REBELLIOUS AMBITION (AKIN TO SUBDIVISION A (1), SITUATION EIGHT)

C (1)—AMBITION AND COVETOUSNESS HEAPING CRIME UPON CRIME

(2)—PARRICIDAL AMBITION

CHAPTER XXXIV

THIRTY-FIRST SITUATION

Conflict with a God

(Elements: *A Mortal; an Immortal*)

Famous usage of this Situation: *Prometheus Bound* (Aeschylus)

THIS situation representing the supreme strife, forms the basis of the greatest dramas of all time. Obviously, its popular appeal is not great, and for this reason it has been rarely used on the screen, except as applied to subdivision A (2),—strife with the believers in a God,—which is usually incorporated in a subordinate and casual capacity. It requires comprehensive treatment and philosophical insight, so that, although it may occasionally be developed in one of its minor phases, as in the story of an atheist's defiance of God, in general, its value is limited.

On the stage, some very powerful dramas have been enacted embracing this situation in one of its nuances. In our memory, however, we cannot recall one that has not been written by other than a master craftsman and for the beginning playwright to attempt to use this situation would probably end futilely.

As stated, the conflict involved in this situation represents the ultimate in human struggle, and due to its spiritual nature it offers little opportunity for physical action. The struggle must arbitrarily be mental or philosophic, inasmuch as we are dealing with a nebulous, unseen, as well as supreme, antagonist. The conflict is decidedly one-sided, as the odds are all in favor of the deity, whether that deity be a mythical God, a carven image of a God, or a religious concept.

We believe it is possible to include in this situation, however, the struggle of a man or a group of people against the members of a religious creed. Such conflict falls under the scope of this situation and no other, so we presume it was Polti's intention to include this type of conflict. Thus, we can include within its realm stories having to do with the heroic faction battling against voodooism, barbaric rites, leaders of cults organized for immoral purposes, and the like. In present-day story creation, this type of conflict offers probably the principal attraction where this situation is concerned.

In classical literature this situation was used to the utmost advantage and a study of mythology will reveal its use in many instances. It has its place in literature, therefore, and a very lasting one. But in our great materialistic world of today, it gains but little credence.

There is one other place where a use might be found for this situation for modern usage, and that is in fantasy. Unfortunately, there is but little demand for this type of material. Even fairy stories for children are frowned upon by most publishers. The majority of them demand that children's stories and books be based on realism. Within the past few years, Walt Disney has done more than any one individual to bring back to children their world of fantasy, and it is to be hoped that his initial movement will bring about a reversion on the part of publishers of children's books and magazines.

It would be to no purpose to endeavor to list any factors for this situation, so we will close this chapter with a list of the subdivisions.

A (1)—STRUGGLE AGAINST A DEITY
  (2)—STRIFE WITH THE BELIEVERS IN A GOD
B (1)—CONTROVERSY WITH A DEITY
  (2)—PUNISHMENT FOR CONTEMPT OF A GOD
  (3)—PUNISHMENT FOR PRIDE BEFORE A GOD
  (4)—PRESUMPTUOUS RIVALRY WITH A GOD
  (5)—IMPRUDENT RIVALRY WITH A DEITY

CHAPTER XXXV

THIRTY-SECOND SITUATION

Mistaken Jealousy

(Elements: *The Jealous One; the Object of Whose Possession He is Jealous; the Supposed Accomplice; the Cause or the Author of the Mistake*)

Famous usage of this Situation: *Cymbeline* (Shakespeare)

THIS situation is of equal value in drama and in comedy. The usual solution offered for "Mistaken Jealousy"—a murder, suicide, divorce, or separation—is extremely hackneyed and undramatic. If this situation is to be used at all, it should be from a fresh angle, or it will lack appeal. It is perhaps more readily applicable in comedy and comedy-drama, than in straight drama, but, because it is so very trite, the student-writer should carefully analyze his use of it in order to determine just how effective it will be in the plot he is constructing.

The student may aptly inquire why the title of this situation should not be simply *Jealousy*. The reason, of course, is that jealousy in itself is not dramatic. We might be jealous of our next-door neighbor when we see him drive up in a beautiful new car and look disdainfully at our old jallopy,—but what of it? However, if we discover that the new car really belongs to a friend of our neighbor's, and that instead of being able to buy a new car the finance company repossessed his car, then we feel a bit superior, as well as sympathetic towards our neighbor. The situation has taken on a certain emotional value.

Although not particularly dramatic and basically much weaker than most of the situations, we must admit that jealousy plays a fairly important role in our lives. It is an emotion experienced at one time or another, or many times, by all of us. It is a natural, human characteristic and therefore belongs in the realm of fiction.

We will list the subdivisions of this situation, in order that the student may see that the most dramatic nuance of it lies in the jealousy of a man or a woman towards the person they love only to find that the jealousy was unwarranted.

A (1)—THE MISTAKE ORIGINATES IN THE SUSPICIOUS MIND OF THE JEALOUS ONE

(2)—MISTAKEN JEALOUSY AROUSED BY A FATAL CHANCE

 (3)—MISTAKEN JEALOUSY OF A LOVE
   WHICH IS PURELY PLATONIC

 (4)—BASELESS JEALOUSY AROUSED BY
   MALICIOUS RUMORS

B (1)—JEALOUSY SUGGESTED BY A TRAITOR
   WHO IS MOVED TO HATRED

 (2)—THE SAME CASE, IN WHICH THE
   TRAITOR IS MOVED BY SELF-
   INTEREST

 (3)—THE SAME CASE, IN WHICH THE
   TRAITOR IS MOVED BY JEALOUSY
   AND SELF-INTEREST

C (1)—RECIPROCAL JEALOUSY SUGGESTED
   TO HUSBAND AND WIFE BY A RIVAL

 (2)—JEALOUSY SUGGESTED TO THE HUS-
   BAND BY A DISMISSED SUITOR

 (3)—JEALOUSY SUGGESTED TO THE HUS-
   BAND BY A WOMAN WHO IS IN LOVE
   WITH HIM

 (4)—JEALOUSY SUGGESTED TO THE WIFE
   BY A SCORNED RIVAL

 (5)—JEALOUSY SUGGESTED TO A HAPPY
   LOVER BY THE DECEIVED HUSBAND

As we review the above subdivisions, the triteness of many of the nuances will become apparent. How many times, for instance, have we come across the story wherein a scorned rival instills in the mind of the fortunate suitor for the hand of the loved one, a feeling of jealousy and distrust, which wrecks the lives of both the fortunate lover and his beloved? And yet, hackneyed as it seems, even this nuance permits of fresh treatment. We would go so far as to say that there is not one single nuance of any situation among the thirty-six that cannot be given novel and distinctive handling.

We believe it will be to the advantage of the student to dwell upon this situation more from the standpoint of comedy. There is something comedic and quite frequently ridiculous about a jealous person and especially if the jealousy is unfounded. On the other hand, there is also something pitiable about an extremely jealous person, and yet it cannot be denied that jealousy is based on distrust, unless the cause is definitely proven, and this has a tendency toward character weakness.

A study of the subdivisions will clarify the meaning of the elements, but so there can be no misunderstanding, let it be said that The Jealous One represents the protagonist. In this situation, however, differing from the others, he is not the initial motivating force. In this case it is in the Author of the Mistake or the Cause, that we find the instigator, or the factor bringing about the initial momentum of the plot. Please notice that we have *four* elements or factors involved in this situation. The second is the Object or the Person of Whose Possession the protagonist is jealous. The third is Supposed Accomplice—practically an innocent victim, inasmuch as he stands accused of doing something of which he is not guilty. And the fourth and last, as stated, is the motivator, The Cause or Author, etc.

The student will find difficulty in working out this "fourth dimensional" situation, and on that account it is deemed advisable to give a few sample plot outlines, rather than attempt to make columnar lists as has been the practice heretofore.

(1)—Let us take as the Jealous One, a husband. The Object of his jealousy is his wife. The Supposed Accomplice is his best friend. The Cause or motivating force is a man in love with the wife; we will call him the antagonist. This antagonist feels that he has a chance of winning the wife if he can get her to divorce her husband. In order to ruin her marriage, he deliberately implants in the husband's mind the suspicion that his wife is carrying on an affair with the husband's best friend. It is true that the friend *does* accompany the wife at times to parties and gatherings when the husband is tied up with his work.

The suspicion implanted in the husband's mind takes root and he commences to mistrust his wife and her attitude towards the best friend. Soon a quarrel ensues between the husband and wife. The antagonist looks on gleefully; his plan is working out.

There are many solutions for such a plot. To make it melodramatic, the husband goes on the "war-path" and decides to kill the best friend. It so happens that the wife, panic-stricken at her husband's sudden denunciation of her actions, goes to the antagonist (The Author) and asks his advice. He becomes importunate and instead of working out his plans subtly, he makes desperate love to her. The husband has followed and comes upon this scene, and the antagonist is neatly drilled with a bullet and gains his just reward for his perfidy. Probably, it would be better to have him live on after being shot, otherwise the husband would be the ultimate victim.

This rough plot outline is given merely for the purpose of indicating to the student the procedure in handling this situation, and not as an example of a novel and interesting plot.

(2)—Suppose we have a dutiful wife as the jealous one. Her husband (The Object) is a producer of burlesque shows. It so happens that the burlesque queen of the show has spurned the attentions of the stage manager (Author or Cause), and he is out for vengeance. He plans a compromising situation for the wife to witness, arousing the latter's jealousy. While witnessing the scene between the husband, wife and burlesque queen, the stage manager falls from the "catwalk" and is seriously injured. He is taken to the hospital. The only thing that can save his life is an immediate blood transfusion. The husband supplies his blood—and the stage manager recovers. He is, of course, grateful for the husband's generous act, and confesses his perfidy.

It is suggested that the student study the subdivisions of this situation and endeavor to use them to work out rough plot formulae such as the above. After some fluency has been developed, it is advised that an attempt be made to combine the situation with one or more of the other situations, and in this way get away from the hackneyed formula which will likely result through the use of this situation as the basis for an entire plot.

greater number of subdivisions listed by Polti under
this situation than in most of the others.

A (1)—FALSE SUSPICION WHERE FAITH IS
          NECESSARY
   (2)—FALSE SUSPICION OF A MISTRESS
   (3)—FALSE SUSPICIONS AROUSED BY A
          MISUNDERSTOOD ATTITUDE OF A
          LOVED ONE
   (4)—BY INDIFFERENCE
B (1)—FALSE SUSPICIONS DRAWN UPON
          ONESELF TO SAVE A FRIEND
   (2)—THEY FALL UPON THE INNOCENT;
          UPON THE INNOCENT HUSBAND OF
          THE GUILTY ONE
   (3)—THE SAME CASE AS (2), BUT IN
          WHICH THE INNOCENT HAD A
          GUILTY INTENTION; IN WHICH
          THE INNOCENT BELIEVES HIMSELF
          GUILTY
   (4)—A WITNESS TO THE CRIME, IN THE
          INTEREST OF A LOVED ONE, LETS
          ACCUSATION FALL UPON THE INNO-
          CENT
C (1)—THE ACCUSATION IS ALLOWED TO
          FALL UPON AN ENEMY
   (2)—THE ERROR IS PROVOKED BY AN
          ENEMY

(3)—THE MISTAKE IS DIRECTED AGAINST THE VICTIM BY HER BROTHER

D (1)—FALSE SUSPICION THROWN BY THE REAL CULPRIT UPON ONE OF HIS ENEMIES

(2)—THROWN BY THE REAL CULPRIT UPON THE SECOND VICTIM AGAINST WHOM HE HAS PLOTTED FROM THE BEGINNING

(3)—FALSE SUSPICION THROWN UPON A RIVAL

(4)—THROWN UPON ONE INNOCENT, BECAUSE HE HAS REFUSED TO BE AN ACCOMPLICE

(5)—THROWN BY A DESERTED MISTRESS UPON A LOVER WHO LEFT HER BECAUSE HE WOULD NOT DECEIVE HER HUSBAND

(6)—STRUGGLE TO REHABILITATE ONESELF AND TO AVENGE A JUDICIAL ERROR PURPOSELY CAUSED

It will be noted that the subdivisions all rely upon false suspicion as the motivating force. Therefore, the subdivisions should not be regarded as forming the entire basis of this situation. The title *Erroneous Judgment,* is the master-key to the situation. Within its scope we may also include *any situation* based upon a wrong interpretation of a circumstance, an unfortunate choice of procedure, an accident caused through miscalculation or lack of skill, misconception of character, and so on. The field encompassed by the situation is far in excess of the nuances of the subdivisions listed.

This situation does not rank among the more powerful of the Thirty-six Situations. Erroneous judgment, mistakes, miscalculations, misconceptions, etc., all indicate a momentary or permanent weakness in character, and where an antagonist deliberately casts suspicion upon an innocent person he loses to some extent his attractiveness as a "villain" because of the subterfuge used instead of direct, clean-cut antagonism.

In this situation it is necessary to have *four* factors:

MISTAKEN ONE	VICTIM OF MISTAKE	CAUSE	GUILTY PERSON
A detective	A crook	Another crook	Second crook's sweetheart
A mother	Her daughter (Accused of wrong)	Mother's sister	The sister
A husband	His wife	Incriminating letter	Woman in love with husband
A banker	His son, (Accused of theft)	Jilted sweetheart of son	Sweetheart's brother

MISTAKEN ONE	VICTIM OF MISTAKE	CAUSE	GUILTY PERSON
A warden	A prisoner (Accused of wrong)	Vengeful convict	Third convict
A girl	Her lover (Accused of murder)	Lover's rival	The rival
A wealthy man	His secretary (An embezzler)	Wealthy man's wife	Wife's lover
Territorial official	Native leader (Accused of revolt)	A white renegade	The renegade
A man	His mistress (Accused of blackmail)	Lover of mistress	Man's wife
A jury	The accused	A lawyer	Lawyer's brother
A judge advocate	Army officer (Accused of being a traitor)	A spy	Spy's sweetheart

The student is apt to find considerable difficulty in adding to this list, because of the somewhat involved elements. There is no clear-cut triad here as in most of the situations. It is necessary to bring in a person motivated by a desire to throw suspicion on an enemy or person he can use as an instrument to attain a purpose. Then we must have the person against whom suspicion is cast. The third element is the person who makes the charges against the victim, or is led to believe he is guilty, and finally, the real criminal or guilty one.

It is suggested that this situation be avoided during the initial period of practice in plot construction, unless it happens to blend with one or more of the other situations. After more skill is acquired, this situation undoubtedly deserves attention and consideration.

CHAPTER XXXVII

THIRTY-FOURTH SITUATION

Remorse

(Elements: *The Culprit; the Victim of the Sin; the Interrogator*)

Famous usage of this Situation: *Crime and Punishment* (Dostoievsky)

THIS situation involves a conflict which is subjective, and therefore of only secondary value for the screen and stage. For these mediums it has frequently been combined with the Second Situation, *Deliverance,* and the Twentieth Situation, *Self-Sacrifice for an Ideal or for Kindred.*

In fiction, a remorseful character has ofttimes been developed advantageously and endowed with real interest. In practically no case, however, can the situation be used as the basis for a novel. For the short story the entire structure can be based on the remorse of a character for a crime or for wrong-doing, and *redemption.*

In this one situation only will we take the liberty of qualifying Polti's Thirty-six Situations. Redemption, as a motivating force, has been omitted from the situations. We believe that it has a true place in dramatic structure, and in all of our study of the situations, this seems to be the only omission.

It might even be possible to add an additional situation, entitled *Redemption,* with the following elements: The Culprit; the Victim or the Sin; Redemption or the Redeemer. The usage of such an additional situation would, of course, involve a crime or wrong perpetrated by the Culprit. The Redeemer or Redemption would be a power, either personal or emotional, to motivate a desire on the part of the Culprit to expiate the crime or sin and redeem himself in his own eyes and in the eyes of the world.

We have hesitated to make this one criticism of Polti's masterly work, but it seems necessary. True, in the first situation, *Supplication,* there is a nuance in which pardon or deliverance is sought, but this hardly comes within the scope of redemption, inasmuch as a person seeking to redeem himself must work out his own salvation rather than find it through supplication of others. He must *earn* his way back into normality and righteousness.

We believe this omission can very well be taken care of by adding an additional element, Redemption. We have then:

CULPRIT	VICTIM	INTER-ROGATOR	REDEMP-TION
Murderer	Hated one	Detective	Gift of life for another

CULPRIT	VICTIM	INTER-ROGATOR	REDEMP-TION
A thief	His employer	The employer	Restitution
A wife (Adulterer)	Her husband	Her mother	Confession to husband
An assassin	A king	Legal authority	Revelation of murderous plot
A politician	A rival	Politician's conscience	Withdrawal from contest
A murderer	His wife	His sweetheart	Suicide
Kidnaper	A child	Detective	Revelation of whereabouts of child
A bandit	Wealthy man	Latter's wife	Restitution
Blackmailer	A woman	Woman's daughter	Pardon sought for wrongdoing
President of Contracting Company	Taxpayers	A catastrophe	Confession and restitution
Business man	His partner	Partner's suicide	Confession and restitution
A rancher	Squatter	Squatter's daughter	Charity
A poisoner	His wife	A vision	Withdrawal of murderous intent

Plot outlines may be rapidly worked out from the above factors, and by recasting the characters and reconstructing the motives, numerous variations may be attained. A mere change in locale and another status for the motivating character will change the perspective.

The human emotion of remorse is a poignant one. It involves such psychological reactions as self-condemnation, sympathy, fear, horror, loneliness, and sorrow. It is obviously a mental struggle, a psychosis brought on through a misdeed or error. The suffering is introvertive and difficult to portray on stage or screen. In fiction it can be used to show the introspective workings of the mind of a remorseful character.

The situation has little to offer for the action type of story. For the "slice of life" story for the literary magazines, it can be used advantageously when combined with our own suggested element, Redemption.

A (1)—REMORSE FOR AN UNKNOWN CRIME
   (2)—REMORSE FOR A PARRICIDE
   (3)—REMORSE FOR AN ASSASSINATION
   (4)—REMORSE FOR THE MURDER OF HUSBAND OR WIFE
B (1)—REMORSE FOR A FAULT OF LOVE
   (2)—REMORSE FOR AN ADULTERY

The classifications under Subdivision A are inherently tragic. Subdivisions B (1) and (2), however, could be used with a "happy ending" in view.

Chapter XXXVIII

THIRTY-FIFTH SITUATION

Recovery of a Lost One

(Elements: *The Seeker; the One Found*)

Famous usage of this Situation: *Oliver Twist* (Dickens)

THE dramatic value of this situation has been almost completely exhausted by very frequent use. Also, it is generally so dependent upon chance, that it fails to produce a genuinely dramatic effect. It forms the basis of all stories about stolen children who are reunited with their parents after many years. It is a situation seized upon by a majority of amateur writers in their early work. For some reason they feel that the mere reunion between parents and children is sufficient to sway an audience.

This situation must not be confused with the Tenth Situation, *Abduction*. This present situation involves exactly what it states—a child or person lost and after either a short or long interval found by the searcher.

Strangely enough, however, no matter how utterly

MEN, WHILE POWERLESS TO PRE-
VENT IT

(2)—HELPING TO BRING MISFORTUNE
UPON ONE'S PEOPLE THROUGH PRO-
FESSIONAL SECRECY

B   —DIVINING THE DEATH OF A LOVED
ONE

C   —LEARNING OF THE DEATH OF A
KINSMAN OR ALLY

D   —RELAPSE INTO PRIMITIVE BASENESS,
THROUGH DESPAIR ON LEARNING
OF THE DEATH OF A LOVED ONE

Subdivision B, *"Divining the Death of a Loved One,"* is rather an interesting nuance. It goes into the realm of fortune-telling spiritualism and astrology, and is the only subdivision touching upon divination. With the constantly increasing number of psychics hanging out their shingles, the subject would seem to offer some interest to the writer at the present time.

Subdivision D is also worthy of note. A person relapsing into primitive baseness through despair on learning of the death of a loved one, suggests a characterization that might be dealt with to advantage if properly handled.

Otherwise, the situation is conventional and has been used time and again in a subsidiary capacity or as a motivation for vengeance.

We must again take some exception to Polti's conception of the elements of this situation. As noted, he lists as elements: A Kinsman Slain; a Kinsman Spectator; an Executioner. Undoubtedly, these elements are ill-conceived, inasmuch as later in the subdivisions it is indicated that the situation does not necessarily involve kinsmen. It does, of course, require the slaying of a loved one, and the heading *Loss of Loved Ones,* must not be construed as coming within the field of Situation Thirty-five, *Recovery of a Lost One,* wherein no death is indicated.

The difficulty in using this situation in any other way than an inceptive or subsidiary situation in a plot, is due to the fact that the Kinsman Spectator is not a character who seeks vengeance against the slayer of the loved one, The Executioner. To use the situation from that angle would be to cast it directly within the scope of the Third Situation, *Crime Pursued by Vengeance.*

In view of the above, it is obviously useless to endeavor to work out any dramatic triads. The situation can only be used in conjunction with one or more of the other situations. The element of the Kinsman Spectator is purely a passive one and remains so within the restrictions of this situation, until he launches forth into pursuit of the *Executioner,* and at the same time entering into the field of Situation Three, as stated above.

* * * * * *

We believe an apt ending for this work would be a quotation from Polti's conclusion to his own compilation of the Thirty-six Situations:

"Thus, I might offer (speaking not ironically but seriously) to dramatic authors and theatrical managers, ten thousand scenarios, totally different from those used repeatedly upon our stage in the last fifty years . . . . . The scenarios will be, needless to say, of a realistic and effective character. I will contract to deliver a thousand in eight days. For the production of a single gross, but twenty-four hours are required. . . . . The situations will be detailed act by act, and, if desired, scene by scene. . . . But I hear myself accused, with much violence, of an intent to 'kill imagination.' 'Enemy of fancy!' 'Destroyer of wonders!' 'Assassin of prodigy!' . . . These and similar titles cause me not a blush."

hackneyed this situation is, it undoubtedly gains some emotional response from an audience or reader, if treated with extreme skill, especially where a child is lost and recovered by the mother.

The beginning writer, however, generally fails to give a novel or masterly touch to the situation and the story ends with the mere reunion of lost one and searcher.

It is advisable, therefore, for the student to use this situation only where it can be blended with one of the other situations and the reunion be a crisis rather than a climax.

It must be conceded that there is dramatic poignancy in the loss and recovery of a loved one, but if the recovery of such a lost one is brought about through coincidence or chance it practically wrecks the dramatic force. A search for a lost one, logically directed and confronted by many obstacles, may lead to an exciting story, especially if the recovery of the lost one has a bearing on other lives.

The situation cannot be used as synonymous with Situation Three, *Crime Pursued by Vengeance,* or the Fifth Situation, *Pursuit.* However, the search for the lost one may be motivated by the necessity of such a lost one's appearing at a trial to save an innocent person accused, providing the lost one is not a criminal. This usage has served admirably in many stories.

In order to render a workable basis for this situation, we will include a third element, Reason for Search.

THE SEEKER	ONE FOUND	REASON FOR SEARCH
A father	A child	Repossession of loved one
	(Trite formula)	
A grandfather	His grandson	Granting of inheritance
A wife	Her husband	Love
	(Hackneyed formula)	
An aviator	Lost explorer	Humanitarianism
A crook	Another crook	To perpetrate a crime
A hypnotist	Hypnotic subject	Money
A husband	An aviatrix	Recovery of loved one
	(Earhart-Putnam situation)	
An art collector	Purchaser of desired art object	Obtaining of object
A detective	A needed witness	Safety of client
A boy	A dog	Love
Man who was kidnaped as a child	His parents	To establish his identity
A man in love	A girl (the beloved)	Restitution for a wrong
A miner	His partner	Discovery of a mine
Tibetan priests	A child	A ruler for country
	(Real life situation)	
A ruler	His son	Establish an heir
An invalid	A derelict	Recovery of lost one

It should be noted that in all of the above triads, an antagonistic force is necessary to evolve a suspenseful plot. A mere search for one lost and success in the search, no matter how dramatic the reason for the search, would have little dramatic value unless the searcher was confronted by obstacles to prevent the recovery from being easy and uneventful.

In working on the elements of this situation, the student should in each case have the searcher confronted by an antagonist who seeks to have the search fail, because the recovery of the lost one would bring about disaster for him. The antagonistic force need not necessarily be confined to the human element. In one of the above triads, the aviator in his search for the lost explorer could be beset by inclement weather, or creatures of sky or earth, to combat his attempt to attain his objective.

We have deliberately neglected to include this fourth and antagonistic element in the above lists, for the reason that we feel it will be to the advantage of the student to draw upon his imagination and evolve an antagonistic force which will tend to create suspense.

Chapter XXXIX

THIRTY-SIXTH SITUATION

Loss of Loved Ones

(Elements: *A Kinsman Slain; a Kinsman Spectator; an Executioner*)

Famous usage of this Situation: *Beatrice Cenci* (Shelley)

WE REGRET that we cannot conclude our analyses of the situations in a burst of enthusiasm for the final one. Unfortunately, it happens to deal with a very tragic theme. Aside from the position in which it normally fits—deep tragedy—it can only be used to advantage as an inceptive situation or one included in a plot which is based on other and happier elements.

Its principal use in modern story writing lies in its suitability for an inceptive situation to murder-mystery stories, where a loved one is slain, motivating the desire for discovery of the murderer and his punishment.

To clarify the meaning of this situation, we will list the subdivisions, before further comment:

A (1)—WITNESSING THE SLAYING OF KINS-

MEN, WHILE POWERLESS TO PRE-
VENT IT

(2)—HELPING TO BRING MISFORTUNE
UPON ONE'S PEOPLE THROUGH PRO-
FESSIONAL SECRECY

B —DIVINING THE DEATH OF A LOVED
ONE

C —LEARNING OF THE DEATH OF A
KINSMAN OR ALLY

D —RELAPSE INTO PRIMITIVE BASENESS,
THROUGH DESPAIR ON LEARNING
OF THE DEATH OF A LOVED ONE

Subdivision B, *"Divining the Death of a Loved One,"* is rather an interesting nuance. It goes into the realm of fortune-telling spiritualism and astrology, and is the only subdivision touching upon divination. With the constantly increasing number of psychics hanging out their shingles, the subject would seem to offer some interest to the writer at the present time.

Subdivision D is also worthy of note. A person relapsing into primitive baseness through despair on learning of the death of a loved one, suggests a characterization that might be dealt with to advantage if properly handled.

Otherwise, the situation is conventional and has been used time and again in a subsidiary capacity or as a motivation for vengeance.

We must again take some exception to Polti's conception of the elements of this situation. As noted, he lists as elements: A Kinsman Slain; a Kinsman Spectator; an Executioner. Undoubtedly, these elements are ill-conceived, inasmuch as later in the subdivisions it is indicated that the situation does not necessarily involve kinsmen. It does, of course, require the slaying of a loved one, and the heading *Loss of Loved Ones,* must not be construed as coming within the field of Situation Thirty-five, *Recovery of a Lost One,* wherein no death is indicated.

The difficulty in using this situation in any other way than an inceptive or subsidiary situation in a plot, is due to the fact that the Kinsman Spectator is not a character who seeks vengeance against the slayer of the loved one, The Executioner. To use the situation from that angle would be to cast it directly within the scope of the Third Situation, *Crime Pursued by Vengeance.*

In view of the above, it is obviously useless to endeavor to work out any dramatic triads. The situation can only be used in conjunction with one or more of the other situations. The element of the Kinsman Spectator is purely a passive one and remains so within the restrictions of this situation, until he launches forth into pursuit of the *Executioner,* and at the same time entering into the field of Situation Three, as stated above.

We believe an apt ending for this work would be a quotation from Polti's conclusion to his own compilation of the Thirty-six Situations:

"Thus, I might offer (speaking not ironically but seriously) to dramatic authors and theatrical managers, ten thousand scenarios, totally different from those used repeatedly upon our stage in the last fifty years . . . . . The scenarios will be, needless to say, of a realistic and effective character. I will contract to deliver a thousand in eight days. For the production of a single gross, but twenty-four hours are required. . . . . The situations will be detailed act by act, and, if desired, scene by scene. . . . But I hear myself accused, with much violence, of an intent to 'kill imagination.' 'Enemy of fancy!' 'Destroyer of wonders!' 'Assassin of prodigy!' . . . These and similar titles cause me not a blush."